W9-CKI-914

Psychological Practice
in Small Towns
and Rural Areas

Psychological Practice in Small Towns and Rural Areas

Robert D. Weitz
Editor

The Haworth Press, Inc.
New York • London

Psychological Practice in Small Towns and Rural Areas has also been published as *Psychology in Private Practice*, Volume 10, Number 3 1992.

The Haworth Press, Inc. 10 Alice Street, Binghamton, NY 13904-1580

Library of Congress Cataloging-in-Publication Data

Psychological practice in small towns and rural areas / Robert D. Weitz, editor.
    p. cm.
    "Has also been published as Psychotherapy in private practice, Volume 10, number 3, 1992" – T.p. verso.
    ISBN 1-56024-280-9 (alk. paper)
    1. Clinical psychology – Practice – United States. 2. Psychotherapy – Practice – United States. 3. Rural mental health services – United States. I. Weitz, Robert D. (Robert Daniel)
    [DNLM: 1. Private Practice – organization & administration. 2. Psychology, Clinical – organization & administration. 3. Psychotherapy – organization & administration. W1 PS86M v. 10 no. 3 / WM 105 P9738]
RC467.95.P79 1991
616.89'0068 – dc20
DNLM/DLC
for Library of Congress
                                                                                        91-35398
                                                                                        CIP

Psychological Practice
in Small Towns
and Rural Areas

Psychological Practice in Small Towns and Rural Areas

CONTENTS

Preface   xiii

Introduction   1
  Robert D. Weitz

Private Practice in Small Towns: New Opportunities
  for Psychologists   3
  Michael F. Enright

  Mental Health Coverage   5
  Social Economic Changes   7
  Small Town Independent Practice:
    A Developmental Model   8
  Conclusion   11

Occupational Hazards of the Rural Psychotherapist   13
  Dotti Cohen

  Entering Into the Rural Community —
    Stages of Community Integration   14
  The Rural Environment   25
  Boundary Problems — The Community/Personal Interface   28

Life in the Slow Lane: An Appalachian Experience   37
  Murray Scher

Small Town Practice of Psychotherapy:
Ethical and Personal Dilemmas   **61**
Suzanne B. Sobel

Staff Problems   63
Personal Issues   65

Anecdotes and Personal Reflections About Psychotherapy
in a Rural Area   **71**
Adrianne C. Kadushin
Lewis R. Kadushin

Historical Development of Our Psychotherapy Practice   71
Factors Affecting the Evolution of Our Practice to Its
   Present Form   74
The Philosophical and Theoretical Basis of Our Practice   78
During a Typical Day . . .   80
What Do We Want to Do When We Grow Up?
   More of the Same   82

Ethics of Rural Practice   **85**
Floyd L. Jennings

Introduction   85
The Development of Ethical Standards   86
Prohibition Against Dual Relationships   88
Special Features of Rural Settings   90
Rural Values   92
Problems with Dual-Relationships in Rural Practice   96
Some Suggestions for the Conduct of Rural Practice   98
Conclusion   103

Practicing Rural Psychotherapy: Complexity of Role
and Boundary   **105**
Dianne L. Sterling

The Increased Attention to Therapeutic Boundaries   112
The Complex Role of the Rural Therapist   117
The Ongoing Nature of the Therapy Relationship   120
The Changed Stance of the Therapist   122

**From Little Acorns Big Oaks Grow: So It May Well Be
with the Practice of Psychology in Small Towns
and/or Rural Areas**   **129**
Robert D. Weitz

Introduction   130
The Story   130

Psychological Practice
in Small Towns
and Rural Areas

ABOUT THE EDITOR

Robert D. Weitz, PhD, a pioneer and innovator in the private practice of professional psychology, has maintained an independent practice for nearly fifty years during his long and distinguished career. He was a prime founder of the Graduate School of Applied and Professional Psychology at Rutgers University and the Florida School of Professional Psychology, now under the aegis of Nova University. At the Florida School of Professional Psychology, he served as the first President and Dean. Dr. Weitz has been honored by the New Jersey State Senate, the New Jersey Psychological Association, the American Society of Psychologists in Private Practice, the American Psychological Association's Divisions of Independent Practice and Clinical Psychology, and has been elected to the National Academies of Practice. He has extensive background as a lecturer and workshop leader, and has presented more than 1200 educational programs to lay and professional groups. Currently, his major therapeutic interest is the application of hypnosis in the treatment of neurotic depression, anxiety states, and psychophysiological disorders. Presently semi-retired, Dr. Weitz conducts a part-time practice in Boca Raton, Florida.

Preface

While the articles included in this monograph should prove to be interesting to psychologists and perhaps members of other professions, it should prove to be particularly significant to the newer and younger psychology practitioners. While there is always room for highly qualified individuals in any location, it is this editor's recommendation to the younger psychology colleagues to follow the advice and concept of Horace Greeley who lived in the days when the United States was beginning to grow and spread out. He advised, "Go West, young man, go West."

Robert D. Weitz

xiii

Introduction

The articles which follow in this monograph were written in response to the editor's invitation. The accounts deal with the experiences of seasoned professionals who have lived and practiced in small towns or rural areas.

The readers will note that while the experiences encountered by the respective authors are frequently similar, there are vast differences which are unique to the practices herein described.

For further information or for reprints of a specific article it is suggested that correspondence be forwarded directly to the author of that article.

Robert D. Weitz

Private Practice in Small Towns: New Opportunities for Psychologists

Michael F. Enright

SUMMARY. Private practice opportunities for psychologists have traditionally existed primarily in large urban areas with large patient pools. Little has been written concerning the current atmosphere for psychologists working on a fee for service basis in small towns. The following discussion reviews current attitudes and needs of people residing in small town America and presents a model for successful practice in this increasingly desirable environment. Advantages to small town practice are discussed and pitfalls in developing a new practice are included.

Because of the rural isolated nature of small town living, many psychologists are unaware that small towns in America offer new opportunities for practitioners interested in private practice (De-Leon, Wakefield, Schultz, Williams & VandenBos, 1989; Enright,

Michael F. Enright, PhD, currently lives in Jackson Hole, Wyoming where he practices with his wife Marilee, a Psychiatric Social Worker. His practice is located in a Medical Arts Building on the grounds of a small general hospital. The building is co-owned and shared by a number of physicians and surgeons.

The author is involved in adult psychotherapy and assessment. He splits his time between individual and marital psychotherapy and conducts psychological assessments for the State Division of Vocational Rehabilitation, the District Court and consulting at the local hospital. He further serves as a Medical Expert for the Social Security Administration.

Dr. Enright and his wife have developed many innovative programs in the small town where they live including a childbirth preparation course. They have also incorporated and operated a private adoption agency and Dr. Enright has been active in national psychological affairs. He is the recent past Chairman of the Board of Psychologist Examiners.

Requests for reprints should be addressed to Michael F. Enright, PhD, 557 East Broadway, P.O. Box 4120, Jackson, WY 83001.

1989). Little is known about the experience of mental health practitioners in small towns. Publications have focused primarily on the problems and experiences of psychologists working in rural community mental health centers (Hollingsworth & Hendricks, 1977; Stuve, Beeson & Hartig, 1989). Many practitioners, however, frustrated by the demands of the bureaucracy in Veterans' Administration Hospitals, county operated mental health centers and other agencies, are leaving the clutter and pressure of the cities to find new challenges and opportunities in small towns. The work of Fein (1983) presents a case study of a psychologist from the New York City area successfully developing a private practice in small towns. Enright (1985) has described the work of the psychologist in conjunction with medical personnel in a small hospital in a rural setting. The ethical issues encountered in a small town child and adolescent practice are presented by Sobel (1984).

A discussion of the demographics and economics of rural America will underscore the need for psychological intervention. Rural communities over the last 40-50 years have been caught up in an economic boom and bust cycle that is tied to the activities of energy companies in the eastern part of the United States, especially in the Appalachian Mountains. Coal companies have left a legacy of unreclaimed land and black lung disease among the inhabitants. This involvement of energy development corporations in small communities has only recently begun in the west where gas and oil exploration and development have caused states like Colorado, Utah and Wyoming to ride an economic roller coaster that depends on the prevailing price of a barrel of oil (McCormick & Turque, 1989). In the heartland of America, radical changes in farming and financing have caused a marked decrease in the ability of the traditional family farmer to survive. Hsieh, Khan, Cheng and Curran (1988) have documented an increase of consumption in beverage alcohol by farmers in response to the "farm crisis."

The following case exemplifies the plight of many long time residents of rural America. A rancher from northwestern Wyoming presented to a psychologist in private practice with complaints of anxiety and depression. He gave an account of a four year duration of watching his crops and animals die, with no apparent cause. The ranch he had lived on had been in his family since his grandfather homesteaded it in the 19th century. Upon further investigation, the rancher found out an oil company had drilled an exploratory well adjacent to his property and that there was good reason to believe that the company had improperly capped the well, causing toxins to enter the aquifer that moved onto his property and made his ground uninhabitable. This man had increased his use of beverage alcohol and had experienced many suicidal thoughts. He had a history of visiting his family physician for anti-anxiety and antidepressive agents. His medical history further showed an increase in blood pressure, peptic ulcer disease, and other stress-related symptoms. He reported he was reluctant to visit the "counselor" in the county where he lived because he did not trust the counselor's ability to keep his private life confidential. Isolated, depressed and alone he only sought help after a referral from his attorney. This man's experience highlights how economic depression brought on by the unstable economy in rural America has been matched by tremendous emotional and psychological upheaval in many cases.

MENTAL HEALTH COVERAGE

The community mental health movement, which began in the early 1960s, and saw its heyday through the middle and late 1970s, affected rural America; although states with low populations rarely met the guidelines for a federal catchment area, federal and state funds did find their way to many communities and the community mental health movement has undoubtedly changed the attitudes and expectations of rural citizens. The most dramatic change in attitude is that many rural Americans now not only have come to accept mental health treatment as important in their lives but have come to expect high quality care for themselves and their families in times of need. The recent changes in health care in America, marked by the development of cost-containment programs, such as HMOs, PPOs and IPAs, have yet to reach rural America, making opportunities for independent practitioners more realistic and less cumbersome.

An important factor for psychologists interested in developing independent practices in rural communities is the reality that there are very few psychiatrists in these communities (State of Wyoming,

1989). There are, however, general practice physicians, many of whom are more than interested in having psychological expertise available to them in the treatment of depressed patients. Independent practitioners can effectively develop relationships with physicians for the treatment of depression and other conditions requiring psychopharmacological intervention. It is keenly important that psychologists in rural areas have an up-to-date knowledge of the types and effectiveness of psychotropic medications. Physicians in rural America prescribe these agents (sometimes with little knowledge) and, once they come to trust the psychological practitioner, they will depend heavily on him for knowledge and the ability to discriminate between psychopathology and iatrogenic side effects of these medications (Enright & Blue, 1989).

Of importance to the rural independent psychologist is the development of family practice medicine. The medical specialty of family practice has been growing since the early 1970s, and a significant portion of the residency programs in American medical schools are aimed at preparing these physicians for rural practice. An equally significant proportion of the residency programs have psychologists involved in the training of family practice residents. The familiarity with professional psychologists often contributes to the positive attitudes found today among family practitioners toward psychologists. To enhance the psychologist/physician relationship the independent practitioner in a small community can affiliate with the local medical-surgical hospital or psychiatric hospital, if one exists. Many community mental health centers in rural states have never accepted nor abandoned the responsibility of emergency intervention, and medical staffs at small hospitals are very receptive to psychologists who are willing to take emergency room calls. Because small hospitals are much less formal than hospitals in urban areas, many opportunities exist that are not found in the city. A psychologist might want to accompany a patient under his care who is scheduled for surgery into the surgical theatre with the surgeon and anesthesiologist. This way he may observe and give support to the patient and anesthesia team during the surgical process, especially if the patient is not having general anesthesia. This willingness to enter surgery can lead to a sense of respect for the psychologist on the part of the surgeon and enhance the rapport between professionals. Anesthesia specialists are, in my experience, very open to psychological consultation in their work and are often surprised and pleased to have a psychologist in surgery.

SOCIAL ECONOMIC CHANGES

The decade of the 1980s has witnessed an increasing social economic shift in rural America. Many wealthy and middle-class families are moving away from the crowded, polluted cities and into the peace, serenity and security of rural communities. Nearly a quarter of Americans live in rural settings and, for the first time, the rural population is growing more rapidly than the urban population. Technological changes have allowed many businessmen and professional people to continue their work effectively while living in and commuting from small towns in rural areas. Perhaps the most important of these changes has been that of telephone communication. The explosion in technology has allowed a person to use a telephone to make connections with almost any other part of the world. Satellite communication has connected rural America to world-wide markets in a matter of seconds. Newer technology, such as "sky pager," allows persons in any part of the country to be connected to the paging system via satellite. Facsimile (FAX) machines allow businessmen to send documents over telephone lines at the speed of light. Computer modem devices put data virtually at one's fingertips. Improved airline transportation has allowed many professionals and businessmen to choose the community of their residence regardless of where their home office is located. In Jackson Hole, Wyoming, for example, there are many airline pilots, business executives, stockbrokers and other high level consultants who travel regularly to the east and west coasts for meetings and business appointments, while maintaining residence in this rural mountain community. Federal Express and other overnight mail services make the site of one's residence or office irrelevant in the day-to-day business activities and responsibilities.

SMALL TOWN INDEPENDENT PRACTICE:
A DEVELOPMENTAL MODEL

Beginning Phase

Psychologists interested in working in independent practice in rural areas must be cautioned that it is extremely difficult to move to a small town and simply hang out one's shingle. This is, of course, difficult in urban areas, but likely more difficult in a small town. Unless the practitioner is accepted as a member of the community, as a person with special expertise, his attempt to develop an independent practice will fail. The following guidelines are suggested in the initial phase of developing a small town independent practice:

1. Assess the community for the need for an independent practitioner. Some more desirable communities are over represented and newcomers are not warmly received in very competitive economic markets.
2. Attempt to develop a contract or part-time employment relationship with existing agencies or human services programs. In the west, psychologists have developed contracts with the Bureau of Indian Affairs, the National Forest Service, the National Park Service, the school systems, and with other state and local agencies. By developing a contract or part-time employment relationship, the new independent provider ensures a steady source of income during the initial phase of getting his/her feet on the ground.
3. Rather than using Madison Avenue type marketing techniques in developing your practice, it is advisable that you develop personal involvement with as many members of the community as possible. This can be done through volunteer relationships on community boards, either as a member or as a consultant; giving continuing education programs to specific groups, such as teachers at the local school or nurses in the local hospital; and teaching programs through the community education programs found in many rural communities. There is no substitute in rural areas for face-to-face interaction with community members and other public relations marketing tactics are

often looked upon as self-serving and meaningless. Old fashioned qualities of trust, dependability and expertise will make the difference in the success of a new private practice.

Transition Phase

The second phase of developing a private practice in a small town is the phase of transition. In this phase, the psychologist moves from a dependent or semi-dependent position to the autonomy of private practice. Practitioners who are establishing themselves in the first one to two years should begin to think about establishing practices that complement other professionals. For example, as mentioned earlier in this discussion, psychologists can successfully consult with medical practitioners in rural areas. Experience has shown that physicians in rural areas fall into two broad categories: the generalists who tend to approach their practice as if they understand everything about the physical and emotional well-being of their patients and the specialists who are highly trained in a specific area of medicine. These practitioners ask for few consults from anyone and are generally not likely to respond positively to a psychological practitioner in their community; and the specialists, who tend to be younger, better trained, and have a more realistic handle on their strengths and weaknesses as practitioners. These physicians tend to be open to psychological practitioners and eager to have another professional with whom they can interact involved in their patients' care.

Those psychiatrists, who can be found in rural areas, are primarily affiliated with private psychiatric hospitals. Independent practice psychologists can develop successful long-distance relationships with those rural psychiatrists. It has been the strategy of large health corporations to completely saturate the marketplace by establishing psychiatric treatment facilities in every region of the country. These psychiatric facilities are, in some cases, quite desperate for referrals and in the interest of good patient care, psychiatrists at the better facilities work to develop referral sources in the communities where their patients live to refer the patient to after discharge from the hospital. Once again, the private psychiatric hospitals are most interested in making these referrals back to independent practitioners, most likely with the assumption that independent practitioners will deliver a better quality of care than can be found at the public clinics.

A final group of professionals that psychologists can complement are attorneys. Many rural states have laws requiring involuntary commitment by physicians or psychologists. Legal professionals are very supportive of psychological professionals who have expertise over and above the average physician in this regard. The traditional forensic psychological needs are great in rural areas and assistance in family law is sought out by many attorneys in rural areas. Obviously, the broader the base of knowledge, the more opportunities the psychologist will have.

The successful independent psychologist in a rural area will have more work than can be accomplished and decisions must be made concerning the specific type of practice in which the psychologist is involved. What follows is a brief summary of the types of opportunities that have been both accepted and declined by the author over the course of a ten year private practice in a rural area.

I have chosen to locate my offices in a medical arts building, which I own with six physicians. I consult to the primary care physicians in diagnosis and treatment of patients with medical/psychological co-morbidity. I am involved with several members of the legal community in personal injury cases. I consult to the National Park Service in the assessment of persons in law enforcement and help train Park Service personnel in emergency psychological services. I work with an air ambulance service (an important part of health care in an isolated rural area) in training EMTs and in intervention in shock and trauma cases. In conjunction with my wife, I have established a private adoption agency to meet the needs of couples who are infertile and young women who have unwanted pregnancies.

I have discontinued working with surgeons for pre- and post-surgery consultations due to the lack of time in my schedule. I am not involved with attorneys in criminal cases nor family law cases, once again because of the time commitment and the stressful nature of this type of practice. Because of the limitations on my time in my practice, I have had to turn down consultations from a local orthodontist who works with TMJ patients and consultations from local chiropractors and other non-traditional medical practitioners. I have limited my practice to the treatment of adults and refer school system requests for assessment and treatment of adolescents and children. Likewise, I refer requests for consultation from human service youth agencies to other services.

CONCLUSION

The current demographic configuration of rural America is such that many people who are suffering economic depression and other psychological problems consequent to the stress of small town life are underserved by psychological providers. Advances in technology are making rural communities available to, and desirable for, wealthy and middle class families interested in leaving overcrowded cities. Psychologists who have been negatively affected by the growth in cost containment, managed health care systems in the city, may be surprised to find new opportunities and desirable personal and professional living arrangements in rural areas. Those practitioners, keeping in mind the developmental model of starting a private practice in a rural area described in this paper, can successfully establish an old-fashioned private practice that is personally rewarding and professionally autonomous.

REFERENCES

DeLeon, P.H., Wakefield, M., Schultz, A.J., Williams, J., and VandenBos, G.R. (1989). Rural America: Unique Opportunities for Health Care Delivery and Health Services Research. *American Psychologist, 44*, 1298-1306.

Enright, M.F. and Blue, B.A. (1989). Collaborative Treatment of Panic Disorders by Psychologists and Family Physicians. *Psychotherapy in Private Practice*, 7, 85-90.

Enright, M.F. (1990). Small Town Independent Practice: New Professional Opportunities. *Psychotherapy in Private Practice*, 8 (1), 3-10.

Enright, M.F. (1985). The Psychologist In Medical Arts Practice and Small Hospitals. *Psychotherapy in Private Practice, 3* (1), 9-21.

Fein, L.G.. (1983). Moving my Practice from Metropolis to Sleepy Hollow. 91st Annual Meeting of the American Psychological Association, Anaheim, California.

Hollingsworth, R.E., Hendrix E.M. (1977). Community Mental Health in Rural Settings, *Professional Psychology*, *8*, 232-238.

Hsieh, H.H., Khan, M.H., Cheng, S.C., Curran, J.J. (1988). Increased Drinking and the Farm Crisis: A Preliminary Report. *Hospital and Community Psychiatry*, 39, 315-316.

McCormick, J. & Turque, W. (1989). America's Outback. *Newsweek, 114*, 76-80.

Sobel, S.B. (1984). Independent Practice in Child and Adolescent Psychotherapy in Small Communities: Personal, Professional and Ethical Issues. *Professional Psychology: Research and Practice 21*, 110-117.

State of Wyoming (1989). Five Year Mental Health Plan, 1989-1993. Department of Health and Social Services, Cheyenne, Wyoming.

Stuve, P., Beeson, P.G., & Hartig, P. (1989). Trends in Rural Community Mental Health Work Force: A Case Study. *Hospital and Community Psychiatry*, *40*, 932-936.

Occupational Hazards
of the Rural Psychotherapist

Dotti Cohen

SUMMARY. This chapter discusses three areas of potential difficulty for rural psychotherapists: adjusting to and gaining acceptance by the community, learning to cope with the rural physical and social environments themselves, and working out the sometimes intricate boundary problems that exist at the personal/community interface. Six stages of integration into rural communities are posited. During the adjustment period, practitioners first deny differences existing in the rural area, then overestimate their ability to successfully integrate. Next they either overidentify with their neighbors, or reject all rural ways. Realizing their strategy is not working, they decide to leave, or to change. If they stay, they can go on to create a workable balance between community pressures and professional and personal values.

Dottie Cohen, PhD, lives on a Hereford ranch in the Sierra Nevada Mountains, on the Nevada-California border. She is Mental Health Director for a rural California county, and is a long-time private practioner in Nevada. She conceptualizes her role in her rural community as that of a participant-observer; filling this role has added many unexpected dimensions to work, and life.

The author's present areas of rural study include: factors contributing to success or failure of mental health practioners and other professionals who have moved to rural areas; the changing nature of rural populations and social structures; how, specifically, rural communities differ from urban and suburban ones; and how therapists can advance their careers even while living in remote regions. Other research interests focus on the problems of the highly intelligent, and various dimensions of lonliness.

When not engaged in professional persuits, Dotti, her husband, and their Akita go adventuring around the western half of the continent, from Alaska to Baja. They are enthusiastic mountaineers, hikers, and explorers of canyons and deserts.

Requests for reprints should be addressed to Dotti Cohen, PhD, P.O. Box 54, Markleeville, CA 96120.

Therapists do not usually consider themselves faced with many hazards associated with their occupation. The ones that do come to mind are the ones from our education and training: errors in diagnosis, selecting an inappropriate intervention, misjudging suicidal or violent intent. Most of us find, once out of school, that doing therapy in the real world is different, and somewhat more complicated, than we initially believed. This fact is doubly true for rural practitioners; not only are there the usual pragmatic issues to be learned, but there are other factors, specific to life in the country, which urban-trained therapists are unlikely to anticipate.

The hazards faced by rural psychotherapists, and unique to them, can be grouped into four categories: entering into the rural community, coping with the rural environment itself, dealing with the personal/community interface, and issues particular to conducting therapy and managing a rural practice. We will take up the first three in this chapter; the last, being quite extensive, is fully examined in a forthcoming book by this author.

ENTERING INTO THE RURAL COMMUNITY – STAGES OF COMMUNITY INTEGRATION

Perhaps you remember the Rosenhan experiment that was published in *Science* in 1973. The researchers admitted themselves to a mental hospital on the pretext they were hearing voices. Once on the ward, they proceeded to behave in a completely ordinary fashion, but the hospital staff continued to treat them as if they were insane. The real patients, however, knew. They would come up to the researchers and say, "What are you doing here? You're not one of us."

Many of us therapists find ourselves in the same situation. We move to the country, adopt a few superficial rural ways, and our urban friends and family think we look genuine, but the real rural people know. They come up to us and say, "What are you doing here? You're not one of us."

They say this sometimes more, sometimes less explicitly. Or we may not hear the words spoken at all, but read it in a glance, in a gesture. This problem is the crux of rural psychotherapy practice (crux meaning not only "central issue" but "something that torments by its perplexing difficulty"). How can we hope to accomplish any substantive work without fitting in to our surroundings? But can we blend in with a culture that is at least partially antithetical to much that most therapists hold dear? And if we do find a way to integrate ourselves, will we go too far — how will we maintain our own individuality?

I have been struggling with these issues for many years, and in talking to numerous other therapists in the rural West, it appears these are problems for most, if not everyone. Some can articulate it, in painful detail, while others just exemplify it. From the therapists I have talked with and observed, and from my own experiences, there are roughly six stages we progress through as more-or-less urban practitioners coming to work in the country.

Stage I. There is no difference between urban and rural practice.

Stage II. There is a difference, but I'll be able to handle it.

Stage III. I'll handle it by becoming just like them, then they'll accept me.

Or:

I'll handle it by being nothing at all like them, and they'll just have to accept me.

Stage IV. This isn't working — I've got to change, or prepare to leave.

Stage V. Leave.

Or:

Start working toward some new balance between the conflicting values and forces; keep learning, make readjustments.

Stage VI. Complete assimilation: frustration ends by adopting community values completely, and abandoning many professional values.

Or:

Live with bearable level of tension and frustration over irreducible conflicts between self and community.

Now to explain a bit more about this sequence:

Stage I. There is no difference. Many of us, and I was one of the guilty, initially believed there was no substantive difference between working in a rural or an urban setting, beyond the obvious factors such as lower population density and fewer social services. I am a good therapist, I reasoned, and know what I am doing. People must have essentially the same problems everywhere, and will respond to the same treatments. I know how to conduct business affairs in the metropolis, so it will just be simpler and easier in the country. I am not going to have a bit of trouble — I'm certain of that. Further, I rationalized, there is probably not that much difference between daily life in the two places. Of course there will not be some of the same leisure time activities, but there will be new ones to take their place. The chief difference is going to be that I will see mountains outside my windows, instead of street lights and parking lots.

Stage II. There is a difference. I'm here in my chosen rural community now, and it appears I was wrong. There *are* differences — big ones and lots of them. Some of them I cannot even describe as of yet, but I keep running into them.

The office I'm in is not up to my standards, but there is nothing else to be found. The telephone system works only intermittently, as does the electrical power. There is a part-time septic tank inspector in the office next to mine, and I can hear him expounding on "tertiary treated effluent" more clearly than I can hear my own patients. It is hard to secure a place to live, and my husband is going to have to make a three hour daily commute to his practice. Everyone seems to think they know all about me, and judging by the stories I hear, most of it is quite wrong.

The people who have been in to see me don't understand the patient role or the therapy process, as I conceive it. They don't want to make appointments — they just drop in any time they feel the need. Some of them don't grasp that they are supposed to talk about their problems, and that I am supposed to ask them questions. They say they "don't want to complain," even though their lives are not going well, and some of them are insulted when I ask personal questions. If I can get them to agree to talk about themselves, many of them lack the experience and language ability to do so. They want me to come to their houses for sessions, which I have never even considered previously. These issues were never mentioned in graduate school. Nothing like any of this has ever come up in the city!

However, I *am* going to be able to handle this, I keep repeating. I grew up in a fairly rural location, and most of my parents' friends were farmers and ranchers. I have a feeling for the country, and I am going to be able to make this work out.

Stage III. I'll be just like them. I have been here for a while now, and I keep having problems. I do what seems best, what always worked when I practiced in the city, and I fail, or it seems people are laughing at me. I don't feel very accepted. What I need to do is to become as much as possible like the locals.

In my case I translated this into acquiring what I thought to be the requisite trappings for life in the West. My husband and I bought cowboy hats and hunting rifles. We got a chain saw so we could gather our own wood. We signed up for country dance lessons, we bought horses, and got riding instruction (far from home, so no one would find out we weren't born knowing how to ride). I thought I was finally on the road to success.

A somewhat related course taken by some newly rural practitioners is that of: *I'll be even better than them.* This also involves therapists attempting to meld with the community, but this time too quickly and completely. They get on every committee, join every group, volunteer for every project. In the struggle to become a necessary part of the community they take on everyone else's responsibilities, promise far more than anyone could deliver, work non-stop on a long list of projects and causes in addition to their therapy, and in general behave like manics. They come to believe they can make everything right for their new community. The lure is there: this is such a small place, and there is so much need — people will really appreciate the many ways I can be of benefit. For these individuals who single-handedly take on the burdens and problems of an entire area, the result is inevitably exhaustion, anger, burnout, failure, and loss of perspective. Oddly, there is also loss of respect from local residents. This sort of behavior is, when properly considered, hubris rather than gallantry. Rural communities have existed, and solved at least some of their problems, for a long while; no person can "fix" all an area's ills, particularly not immediately and all alone.

An alternative possibility, a path taken by many other individuals, is:

Stage III. I'll be nothing at all like them. The persons represented here are having the same experiences, of nothing they try being successful, and feeling unaccepted. But these therapists conclude the best plan is to reject everything rural and maintain their urban identities completely unchanged. The community, these individuals reason, will just have to get used to me as I am. In the therapists I have observed personally, this has been the more common pattern for the newly transplanted. One woman, in the face of community disapproval of her lifestyle, found and began dating a Black man (not always an easy feat in the rural West). She was not very attracted to him as a person, but believed it would scandalize her neighbors, and she was correct about that. Another took to wearing a diamond in her pierced nose, and openly using illegal drugs. Some rigidify their therapeutic styles, and if that doesn't suit their patients, they are not particularly concerned. Other therapists retreat into speaking entirely in psychological jargon, and use it as a weapon against those who do not understand it. The community perceives this type of behavior as either acting "better than," which is resented, or interpreted as simply not caring about local residents' sensibilities.

Stage IV. This isn't working. After a time the realization comes to you: your strategy is not working. Either strenuously avoiding any assimilation, or rushing to change identities wholesale has not solved the problems you first experienced, and has now created new ones. In my situation, the horses were far more expensive and troublesome than I had guessed, and I had no natural talent at riding. I lugged the rifle up mountains and down ravines, never did find anything to shoot, and rather hoped I wouldn't. We didn't really want to spend every weekend cutting wood, and couldn't develop an appreciation for country/western music. The locals were still laughing at me, rather scornfully by now, and I was still not feeling part of the community.

Colleagues I have observed taking the other path, that of rejection of all things rural, encounter professional malfunction and acute unhappiness even sooner. I appeared foolish to the residents, and felt personally ill at ease and somewhat inauthentic, but at least people were coming to me for services, and I was having some success working with local agencies and groups. The devoutly urban therapists are, by this point, the recipients of considerable community animosity, even hostility. Local residents are openly wondering what these people are doing in the community, why they came here, and taking bets on when they will be gone. Most persons avoid contact with them if at all possible. The therapists themselves are usually feeling bitter, misunderstood, and unappreciated. In either case, the conclusion is: this isn't working. I must either change, or prepare to leave.

Stage V. Change, or leave. Many would-be rural therapists do leave at this point. And not just the group who refused to assimilate. Some individuals, who have tried so hard to accommodate themselves, and still feel rejected, get discouraged and decide it isn't worth the continued struggle. Rarely is it possible for a professional to depart abruptly, so there is usually some elapsed time between the decision to move away and the actual decampment. During this period a few individuals experience relief, feeling they are going on to a situation more in accord with their style. For most, however, it is an awkward time, since they now have no illusion of commitment to the community, and find working there almost intolerable.

Those who leave at this point are a cause for sadness. First, not only has the community failed to benefit from the skills and knowledge of the therapist who left, but it has also had its negative beliefs confirmed. Most rural residents have distorted views of mental health professionals, intellectuals, city dwellers, and outsiders in general. This is just one more example they can point to supporting their assertions that "those people " cannot be relied on, and makes it even more difficult for the next practitioner they meet. Second, the therapists leave with a failure experience, and probably a dent in their professional confidence and self-esteem. They also leave with a negative and inaccurate image of rural people. I advise colleagues who are feeling that practice in the country does not suit them to stay at least until they achieve some small, personally meaningful success, or until they believe they have learned something beneficial to themselves. This may result in their deciding to remain indefinitely, but that is not the purpose. The aim is for them to achieve a more natural closure with their experience, and to lessen the perception of failure.

But others, happily quite a few others, start working at this juncture toward real resolutions of the dilemma. They make new mistakes, of course, but they keep learning and readjusting. In my case I began looking at my community as if I were an anthropologist in a strange land. I started to notice what really mattered to the long-time residents. I found that no one cared if I could dance the "Cotton-Eyed Joe," or if I owned a horse. Most of them didn't, either.

What my rural neighbors cared about, really cared about, were issues few in number but broad in scope. One, they wanted me to be able to take care of myself, to be fairly independent and self-reliant. In isolated communities with few resources, what no one wants is a new person who is needy and helpless. They didn't care if I had cowboy boots, they just thought I needed something warm and sturdy that would keep the snow out. They wanted me to be able to drive around without getting stuck twice a day and forcing someone to stop and help me (because in rural areas you never pass by someone you know to be having problems). My vintage Porsche was an object of admiration by many in the city where I used to live — out in the country it was a source of much head-shaking. Why, everyone wondered, does she drive a car without much of a heater and with only a few inches of ground clearance when she needs to travel up and down unplowed dirt roads through mountain winters?

Two, they wanted me to feel and express some commitment to the area. Even a real estate agent asked us, in our first month in the community, how committed we were to staying there. They expected I would ask and begin learning about local history, geography, economics, resources, and problems. They wanted to tell me about the old families, most with current descendents, who had settled the area. While they wanted to hear about my family, they didn't care to hear how things were done back in the city. They quietly hoped to see signs that I was abandoning some of my urban ways.

Third, they wanted to see me decipher and begin operating on the prevailing rural ethic. This included points such as getting to know everyone's automobile, and waving to them whenever we passed. It entailed not taking favors for granted, not incurring debts, not expecting local people to do things I was not willing to do myself. Most of all it revolved around the above mentioned self-reliance.

Finally, while they only hoped they would not have to take care of me constantly, they were delighted when I decided to do something to help care for the community by becoming a volunteer emergency medical technician. You might think being a therapist already meant I was helping the community, but there is a different slant put on helping in a rural area. Every able bodied person is expected to have a job, and everyone's job is in some way helpful to the entire community, whether that is being a snow plow operator, running the cafe, being a deputy sheriff, or a psychotherapist. In addition, the most esteemed members of the community perform some other volunteer service, generally unrelated to their principal work. The school superintendent did search and rescue work. A janitor was a reserve deputy sheriff. One of the deputies had a band that played for free at community events. The tow truck driver was a volunteer fireman. It is not simply a matter of pressure toward altruism — in isolated rural communities there is not sufficient money or persons to fill all needed posts. If many do not volunteer, much remains undone. My being an EMT both facilitated and complicated my therapeutic interactions, but most significantly, it was valued by the community.

Stage VI. Complete assimilation, or cope with it. Therapists who choose to remain in rural areas, and who go through the often lengthy period of reassessing and readjusting in Stage V, are understandably quite tired by now. Making matters worse, there appears never to be an end in sight. For most, the tensions, conflicts, and frustrations lessen, but never disappear. For the majority it becomes apparent, for reasons soon to be described, that they cannot go away entirely. Yet a rare few do achieve a total solution of sorts.

The solution never consciously adopted but sometimes "drifted into" is that of total assimilation into the rural community. This is something akin to anthropologists "going native" — when the Land Rover or the bush plane returns for the scholar, he or she cannot be distinguished from the tribe being studied, and does not wish to, or is no longer able to, return. In this scenario, the former urban therapist slowly blends in with the community, casting off bit by bit the previous identification with professional standards and concerns. Community values and perceptions become increasingly and unquestioningly their own values and perceptions.

This is not a mysterious process. One way of understanding it is to consider how such change reduces painful dissonance within individuals. Conflicts arise between how therapists believe they should be conducting themselves, and the way in which the community wishes them to behave. They try and fail to change the community, but if they change themselves, and come closer to community standards, there is less conflict. A second way to understand it is simply in terms of reinforcement. The censure and approval of neighbors and co-workers is usually a powerful force in the lives of most persons, but that power is heightened within the confines of a small, isolated community, where neighbors and co-workers are often one and the same. Obviously, it is reinforcing to feel less frustration and tension, and not to have neighbors angry with one. As I have said, people aren't aware of this process, and do not consciously select it for themselves. But former colleagues are many times shocked when they encounter a therapist they knew years before who now seems so different.

A man of my acquaintance took this path. He came from a metropolitan area, where he had been both a teacher and a social worker. At first he encountered the same difficulties we all do, such as lack of acceptance and understanding by the community. But gradually, incrementally, he became one with the social structure of his isolated town. He would gamble in the local Friday night poker games whether or not they included his patients. While he often used his position to help patients avoid prosecution, other times he would merge his role with that of law enforcement by assisting deputies in stakeouts and arrests. Though he sometimes curried favor with his patients by bringing them liquor, nonetheless he would later discuss their personal problems with his fellow "good old boys" at the coffee shop. He offered to be a substitute teacher at the grade school, and instead of teaching the lessons of the day, would tell ribald stories about community citizens, and tall tales regarding local history. In short, he surrendered all professional ethics, and several of his former personal standards, in order to fit in. Up until the time that ill health and the culmination of some major scandals forced him to retire, he seemed quite blissfully happy in his work, and is now enjoying a jovial retirement.

Fortunately, this is not the course followed by most rural practitioners. I cannot say if one would not perhaps be "happier" following the above path. But what happens for most of us, what occurred for me, is that we continue to live with bearable levels of tension and frustration over irreducible conflicts between professional self and community.

Why is this conflict so inevitable? From my observation, it does not depend very much on the particular characteristics of the town or the individual. It arises because of the nature of the systems and structures of both psychotherapy and rural communities. The values, beliefs, expectations, and world views of most professional psychologists are fundamentally at odds with those of most isolated rural communities. This topic alone could be the subject of a paper, and I have space for but a few brief examples.

Therapists are taught to value the confidentiality of their patients above almost all else; rural persons feel if you have some information that may provide enlightenment or amusement for your neighbors, you have an obligation to share it. Conversely, psychotherapists of every persuasion ask their patients to discuss freely personal concerns and problems, and expect to help them in the solution of those problems; rural people admire those who keep their worries to themselves, and take care of their own difficulties without involving outsiders. While therapists are taught to live with and think in terms of ambiguity, rural dwellers have little toleration for it, and want clear cut answers. Most psychologists are professional optimists by training—we always want to believe change is possible, and good; rural people frequently lack a strong belief in either the possibility or the desirability of change.

Many psychotherapists were born in and grew up in or near urban areas. Even those who initially lived in the country spent considerable time in the university-town environment obtaining necessary education and training. Most internships are available in metropolitan regions. There is the enculturation of graduate school itself. One of the purposes of most professional education is not just to impart facts and methods, but attitudes and ways of seeing the world—this is at least as true for psychology as for other disciplines. All of the above serves to make rural persons suspicious of therapists, and causes therapists to feel they have stepped into another world when they come to practice in the country.

A final factor in the conflict between rural practitioners and their communities is that of reference groups. In isolated rural areas, the community *is* the reference group for all who live in it. For most persons, no others are available — should another be possible, one is expected not to include oneself in it. However, most therapists feel they belong to the larger society of practitioners, and psychologists in general, at the regional and national levels. This is conveyed, more or less explicitly, to the rural community, who in turn feels betrayed and devalued. The community rule is that no one will have strong outside allegiances, and yet the professional serves as a reminder that some obviously do.

It wasn't until I grasped this unwritten code that I understood the outraged reactions I occasionally experienced. An assertive elderly woman came to my office and, after the briefest social interchange, asked how Sally was getting along in therapy, what she generally talked about, and if she was plotting to divorce Jim and take his money. I was completely shocked — I refused to acknowledge if Sally even was in treatment, and said that I could not release the sort of information she was requesting. She informed me that she was the sister of Sally's mother-in-law, and was therefore entitled to know. In fact, she demanded to know. I told her I was sorry she was not getting what she wanted, but I would not divulge confidential information. "You tell me why exactly not, young lady," she snapped. "Because," I said, as calmly as I could, "I'm a psychologist, and psychologists don't do things like that." This totally outraged her. Not only did I have an outside reference group, but I was telling her that in this case such a group had a stronger influence on my actions than did the rural community where I was living. "And you," she shot over her shoulder as she stormed out, "you try to call yourself an Alpiner! Hah!" ["Alpiner" being a real resident, as opposed to a tourist or a seasonal visitor, of Alpine County.]

And so there are those of us who have made it to Stage VI, incompletely assimilated — probably always will be — but still committed to a rural practice. During the less good times we feel the same painful conflicts we experienced in our first months in the country, and despair that it still has not improved. We wonder what we are doing here. Yet on the good days we find some humor in the farce and folly of our situations; perhaps we even relish the ambiguities and the simultaneous ambivalence we feel. And we know, without having to say it, that this, for now, is a good place for us to live and work.

THE RURAL ENVIRONMENT

Having achieved some sort of entry into the rural community, practitioners at any of the above stages are likely to encounter additional hazards in both the environment itself and in establishing the boundaries between themselves and their communities.

There exist several definitions of what constitutes a rural area. The U.S. Census Bureau has probably the most liberal classification: by their tally fully 25% of the population and 75% of the counties in this country are rural. I, and I suspect many of the other writers in this monograph, have more stringent criteria in mind. As opposed to an urban-rural dichotomy, I think of varying degrees of ruralness. There are communities within a 15-20 minute drive from mid-sized cities that are peppered with convenience stores, small shopping malls, and a wide variety of services, and while some of the residents may consider themselves rural, they are not genuinely rural. Carson City, the capital of Nevada, has a population of approximately 35,000 persons, and calls its community mental health center a "Rural Clinic" (its officially designated name). Clearly these places would be rural compared to San Diego, but they are seen as almost big cities from the perspective of, say, Roscoe, Montana.

The places of interest to me, and those of principal concern in this chapter, are the truly rural, isolated communities. They are distinguished foremost by their geographic features and their distance from any large city, or even from any major transportation routes. Most of the examples of this type of community, particularly in the American West, are actually located at considerable distance from other population centers—it is not just a matter of perception, or of felt distance. The people of Bridgeport, California make a six hour round trip drive to go shopping or get to medical specialists in Reno, Nevada, the closest large city to them. Major highways are nowhere near many of these communities. Indeed, some of them were more populous and thriving before the advent of the Interstate Highway system. In addition, there are generally some isolating geographic factors. Many truly rural communities are high in the mountains, far out in the desert, across several treacherous mountain passes, located on narrow, twisting, inadequate roads, or cut off at times due to avalanches or flash floods.

These isolated, genuinely rural communities have some very different characteristics, including an older, poorer, less educated population, a narrower and more precarious economic base, and a lower level of overall prosperity. There is more substandard housing, and far worse availability of services, including medical and mental health care. The total of all of these factors helps form the strikingly different beliefs, attitudes and lifestyles adopted by residents, and results in therapists having difficulties living and working comfortably in these places.

To begin with, there is usually a harsher environment to be dealt with. As was discussed earlier, most new rural practitioners have recently come from urban areas, where the forces of nature are kept partially at bay. Where I live some roads are snow shut completely in winter, others subject to avalanches periodically trapping people on one side or the other, rivers flood over roads in the spring, forest fires rage in the summer, extreme winds sand blast paint off cars, bears pillage the trash, mountain lions eat dogs, eagles carry off kittens, deer collide with automobiles—all in all, people have a chance to interact with the natural world a great deal. Sometimes a great deal more than they would like. These situations alone can be quite taxing to a newly transplanted professional, especially if he or she was concentrating chiefly on the concerns of setting up a practice in a new location.

Then there is the social environment with which to contend. Some newly rural therapists experience it as being at least as hostile as the weather. Any of several personal characteristics can contribute to new arrivals experiencing difficulties. Being young relative to the rural population is a handicap. Younger people in professional roles find it harder to be perceived as knowledgeable, or competent. Belonging to a racial, ethnic, or religious group with which the community has had little experience, or which is disliked, can be a source of considerable difficulty. Likewise being female and attempting to function outside the few prescribed roles for women (mother, teacher, secretary, waitress, or nurse) can have negative repercussions. Some persons, women as well as men, will actively dislike the non-traditional woman, while most rural residents will just fail to take her seriously. Such attitudes can cause problems for practitioners of both sexes — female therapists are expected to be nurturing, compassionate, and perpetually available for the community's needs, but are not seen as real experts of any sort; male therapists are expected to have immediate, exact answers to everyone's problems, and to be paragons of strength.

Rural people do not hold these opinions out of sheer perversity. In most isolated communities there has been little opportunity to correct either mistaken notions handed down from previous generations, or beliefs based on limited, idiosyncratic experience. All of us who remember our social psychology can understand how difficult it is to change attitudes and beliefs in the face of little evidence to the contrary. In that situation, the very few counter-examples can be dismissed as anomalous, and the belief persists unchanged.

When I first moved to my community, I was attempting to convince a group of locals that their prejudice against Black persons was incorrect. I told them of the Blacks I knew in the city of both average and extraordinary accomplishments. Then a Black man came to the community. He moved in with an Indian woman, fathered a child he refused to support, got arrested for driving while intoxicated, and broke into the truck of the Sheriff's son to steal his hunting guns. He was incarcerated outside the area. The group whose attitude I was attempting to alter came to me and said, "See?" In the years since, no other Blacks have come to live here, and the negative stereotype persists unabated.

Similarly, there are few women in responsible positions here. When one of them does a credible job handling a difficult situation, this does not draw much comment. However, when a woman has problems with her employees, becomes overly emotional in public, or quits working, saying she cannot handle the pressures, people nod their heads sagely. We notice that which confirms our expectations.

An elderly rural woman saw me running along the highway, and cautioned me that "women weren't meant to run" — I was going to damage myself. I told her of the thousands of women who routinely run marathons, and she simply didn't believe me. It wasn't until I was able to call her attention to a televised marathon with numerous women competing that she would allow such a feat might be possible; she still reserved judgement as to its desirability.

On the positive side, most rural people will, after a time, come to value sincere, knowledgeable professionals despite their initial prejudices. Patience, persistence, and non-stridency are eventually rewarded with at least some measure of acceptance.

A final environmental hazard of rural practice is the difficulty in finding a satisfying social circle. In urban areas most of us maintained a diverse network of personal relationships. When I moved to the country I expected some professional isolation — I knew there would not be many other colleagues for mutual support or consultation. However, I was not anticipating the paucity of non-professional, personal relationships. This situation is not simply a function of fewer people overall; research tells us we make and keep friends more easily when they are similar to us in a few salient dimensions. There are few individuals in remote rural locations who are similar to most therapists in personal characteristics and interests. Many rural colleagues tell me, and I find this true myself, that their best friends, the ones from whom they feel the most genuine understanding, live outside their communities, and often quite far away. As a consequence they see them less often, and have not found suitable replacements closer to home.

BOUNDARY PROBLEMS — THE COMMUNITY/PERSONAL INTERFACE

Awhile back I arrived at the elementary school, where I do therapy with some students who are having problems. The school secretary, who is new to the area, ran across the parking lot to meet me, and said my husband was on the telephone, looking for me. I asked her why she thought it was him. "Well, he called just as you were driving up, he said he knew you would be coming here at this time, and he described either of the two cars you would be driving. Who else could it be?" "Almost anyone who lives around here," I replied. Indeed, it was a new patient who had forgotten what time his appointment was for the next day, and knew I would be going to the school that afternoon, because everyone knows that, and knew both my cars, because everyone knows that, too. The secretary was thoroughly amazed. If you have lived in a small community for any length of time, you are not surprised at all.

Everyone knows everyone in rural areas. This is particularly so for more public figures such as therapists. There is some knowledge acquisition that occurs passively — people observe us often enough to form conclusions about parts of our lives we normally may not share. But for prominent persons, and psychologists are sufficiently unusual to rate that label in the country, some residents take a delight in actively seeking out information about them. I hear citizens excitedly carrying bits of information to one another as trophies or gifts, regarding the new Post Mistress or the man who may run for Sheriff. Such exchanges serve to bind the community socially, as well as keep everyone informed.

As a result, therapists are especially scrutinized. I cannot say whether it is more annoying to have everyone know factual details of my personal life, or to have them "know" that which is not true. Some believe they know all about me because they talked to me at a meeting, because they are friends with someone who lived next to me, because they know someone who has seen me professionally, or because they have seen me themselves. [This is the obverse of confidentiality — I cannot say anything about them, but they can give opinions on me, even after one session.]

This aspect of rural life is extremely unnerving to newly transplanted urbanites. Some rural colleagues I talk to find it hard to believe that everyone seems to know their work schedule, their fees, where they live, and with whom, what they like to do with their free time, their religion or lack of it, whether their parents are alive and if they get along with them, and just about anything else you could imagine. There seems to be little use in attempting to counteract this situation. Telling people that something is none of their business makes them angry, and they do find out what they wanted to know, in any case. Certainly practitioners who have more conventional lives will be at an advantage; those with more flamboyant or unusual lifestyles will require a thicker skin.

The really negative, though fortunately rare, result of your life being on public display occurs when a patient or relative of a patient develops an urge to threaten you. This has been a serious worry only twice during many years for me, but such a situation is, needless to say, quite unpleasant. In one instance an abusive mother concluded I was to blame for her child being removed by Social Services, and in the second case an abusive husband believed I was attempting to get his wife to leave him. Both times the individuals let it be known they were considering coming to my house and doing me great bodily harm. However, while living in a tightly interwoven community allowed the threats to take on more real proportions, it also counteracted their likelihood of being carried out. Yes, the threateners knew exactly where I lived and what my schedule was, but I was easily able to get the message back to them that I would not passively allow myself to be victimized, and to inform them that everyone knew what they were saying. A more dangerous situation could arise if a patient with hostile intentions told no one of his or her plans, so the community could not help dampen the threat.

A far less serious, although quite aggravating fact of rural practice is the difficulty of establishing boundaries between work time and time off. If you are a workaholic therapist, of course, you can have trouble with that issue no matter where you live — the uniquely rural problem is getting your patients to acknowledge your privacy and your personal time. This is not a problem suffered by rural psychotherapists alone: physicians, ministers, attorneys, and law enforcement personnel, among others, face similar challenges. We all know if we do not have sufficient time completely away from work we become less and less productive when we are at work, and yet it can seem almost impossible to really get away. After you have lived in a very small community for some time, almost everyone you encounter when you leave home is a patient, former patient, friend or relative of a patient, or someone who wants to "talk shop" with you. A quick trip to the general store for a carton of milk can turn into a two hour trip replete with advice giving, follow up, and crisis intervention. I keep working on setting limits, and occasionally get people angry with me, but it has slowly changed for the better.

Related to this, for those therapists who worry about such things, it is hard to uphold a professional image. Patients and potential patients encounter you everywhere, and not always in the most flattering circumstances. Some just meet you with surprised and critical looks, while others will let you know they expect you to behave differently than you may wish to. This was a cause for frustration and angst for me in the beginning, but I have learned to laugh to myself about it over the years. Invariably, as I am running down the highway in neon purple lycra tights and a tank top that reads: "Asics — the choice of fanatics," or when I am returning from a several-day backpack covered with mud, scratches, and bug bites, the very primmest and stuffiest community members will encounter me and coolly eye me up and down. I smile jovially and say something cheery. I haven't been doing anything illegal or immoral, and we just can't live up to everyone's expectations, can we?

Sometimes, instead of others attempting to make you squirm, it is your presence that makes them uncomfortable. I have had to combat guilty feelings after appearing in some places, since I seemed to be ruining someone's evening. As with many rural areas, most people in my community have a post office box to receive their mail. Occasionally, I will find myself going to the Post Office at an atypical time, such as Saturday night, not having done it earlier. Our Post Office is diagonally across the main intersection in town from the only bar, where some locals spend more time than would be advisable. It happens fairly often, especially on warm summer nights, that I will be startled by someone running up to my car in the dark saying, "I was only in there having a Pepsi!" or, "I just went in there looking for my sister!" I say, "Look, I'm not your mother. You do what you wish. I was just getting my mail, and had no idea you were here until you came running over to me." A similar effect can occur at public meetings, where I have come only as an interested citizen, not in any "official" capacity, but nevertheless cause some individuals to evidence discomfort, especially if they are getting overly-emotional. Some current and former patients are horrified to encounter me in public, even though they must know they will in such a small place. They look for all the world as if they believe I am going to blurt out details of their sex life as we stand around the unleaded pump.

The above can also serve as examples of the larger, all-pervasive problem of role overlap in tiny communities. There are simply not enough people to provide that buffer of "strangers" we are so used to in urban areas. It is rare, in even mid-sized cities, to encounter current patients outside one's office – it is a daily occurrence in the country. And we not only encounter them, but find ourselves in some additional relationship with them. In fact there is a great possibility, with each of your patients, that you have had or will have some other sort of non-therapy interaction – as if the relationship of patient and therapist were not complicated enough.

My community is so small I feel I cannot ethically give explicit examples of the convoluted, sometimes hilarious, often anxiety-provoking cross-connections between myself and patients/community members. I have treated prominent persons. I have treated notorious persons (that the community would rather see hanged than helped). I have had to commit involuntarily, or cause to have arrested, individuals the rest of the town lionized. I have had former patients or their family members attain positions of power, and then either live in fear of me, or try to subtly threaten me, worrying our former relationship would be revealed.

Similarly, I often find myself appointed to committees and boards of various sorts, there never being sufficient volunteers for all the needs. Many times patients and former patients come before these same bodies, needing help or requesting some consideration. They may be competing for scholarships, applying for jobs, or having problems with their child's school attendance. What they have in common is they generally expect special understanding from me, since I am their former therapist. Making objective decisions under such circumstances is terribly difficult, but there is no good way out, once the situation has presented itself. When Mary Smith unexpectedly comes before the interview panel on which I am serving, I cannot say I will be unable to vote on her – that would be tantamount to saying she is my patient. Worse yet, the rural ethic calls on me to do all I can to help this person over someone I do not know as well, or who is not as needy, and so there is a belief that those I do vote for or support must be patients.

A last, and especially vexing, problem for those of us who are mere mortals, is that therapists are expected not to have their own problems. Some city dwellers may believe this as well, but they do not get to know their therapists as rural people do, and generally do not know if their therapists have personal problems or not. This is a fate shared by other rural professionals, to some extent, but somehow therapists feel it the most. We are usually put on a far higher pedestal than feels comfortable, and it is such a long way to the ground if we slip.

Woe to the rural marriage counselor whose own relationship experiences rocky times, or to the rural family therapist whose child is not perfect. Are you feeling depressed, or going through an anxious period? Half the community will make snide jokes about it, the rest will be horrified, and everyone will doubt your competence somewhat. People will expect that you should never have too much to drink, make a foolish purchase, develop insomnia, quarrel with a neighbor, or even be in a bad mood for no visible reason. Most rural people will genuinely expect that you are much closer than they to having life figured out, and being able to handle all situations perfectly. When you fail, you disappoint them, and also frighten them to some extent. If the doctor can get sick, what hope is there for the rest of us to stay well?

Two years ago my husband and I returned from a backpack trip to find our home, cars, and everything else we owned destroyed completely by a major forest fire. It also burned down a large percentage of the other homes in my town. We arrived two days after the destruction, and of course the community was still in shock. We were in shock. Had I not been so profoundly affected, I would have done what I could to provide disaster-related mental health services to the residents, but I simply was unable. The Red Cross, seeing I was one of the needy, instead of a potential helper, brought in two therapists from outside. Absolutely no one would talk to them. At a time such as that, no rural person wanted to be dealing with strangers.

I discovered the devastation on a Friday afternoon, and was back at work on Monday morning. I felt an obligation to be strong, and to provide services as best I could. It seemed to me at the time I was functioning fairly well, but in retrospect I realize I was rather marginal. It was hard to focus on conversations, I burst into tears without warning, and felt overloaded by even small additional setbacks.

Just when it seemed I felt as bad as possible, people began telling me I had to be better, and had to do so immediately. Intuitively, I knew everyone was expecting me to be a model of strength and cheerful calm. I knew they did not want to see me grief-stricken and seriously depressed, and I was trying to oblige, but now people were coming to me and telling me explicitly that I was not doing enough. They didn't want me to do anything directly for others, necessarily, but they were demanding I be a model of fortitude. I was to cease feeling hopeless and weak and in pain.

About one week post-fire, an acerbic elderly woman who had also lost her house approached me in the bank, where I must have been looking less than well. She barked out, "Look at yourself! Come on, you big head-shrink with all the fancy degrees, if you can't snap out of it, what are the rest of us gonna do? You're s'posed to be showin' us how to handle this!" Foolishly, I redoubled my efforts to appear impervious, and believed I was being successful. Predictably, this behavior resulted, several months later, in fairly severe physical problems, caused by the repressed and unresolved emotional distress.

This has been my most recent major lesson about rural life and practice. The community is correct — I am a model, and a highly visible one at that. There is no denying it or escaping it. But I refuse to be an idealized, flawless one. The model I now aspire to is that of a human being, albeit one with some specialized training and experience, who is trying her very best, but sometimes failing, to cope with the vagaries of life. If it disappoints some people, I regret that, but perhaps it is healthier for them after all, than to see me trying to emulate a saint. I know it is certainly healthier for me.

I'm not generally a night owl, but tonight I am sitting up late, finishing this chapter. The rest of the county is in bed by now, even the late-shift deputy. The moon, one day away from full, is reflecting in the duck pond across a field from my front door. A few restless cows are calling out, and now and then, faintly, there is the rumble of a lonely truck way out on the highway. I'm in a small house with green shutters and a white board fence, on a cattle ranch, at the exact spot where the Great Basin meets the Sierra Nevadas. Just to the west, the Sierras rise more than a mile straight up above me, and to the east the Basin and Range province takes off, going for over five hundred miles without cease. I sit here in the stillness, wondering at the events that have brought me here, and at all that has occurred since. What can I say, with some certainty, about my years of practice in this community?

There have been intensely joyful times here. I have done some of the best work of my life, and had few to observe it. There is no doubt this has often been a difficult and sometimes painful place, both personally and professionally. I know I have learned a great deal. Have I learned enough to account for the years I have spent? I hope so. I know I have alleviated much suffering, provided some inspiration, guided many youth, helped a few people die at peace, prevented some tragedies, advanced the cause of psychology where I could, and in recent times, tried to provide a *real*, human, role model for those in search of one. I have had great independence thrust upon me, and fortunately, I like it. Rural practice impels one to be creative, to improvise, and to grow stronger and more self-reliant.

Would I do it all again, given the choice? Fortunately, we are not faced with those sorts of decisions, but I think I would. This time without quite so many mistakes, please. Not that there aren't times I fantasize about doing research at a major university. . . . But this is home — the whole of the rural West is home. You know the place is home when it starts to break your heart, when you start worrying about what is happening to the land, to the social structure. This is home more deeply and fundamentally than the city of my birth.

Will I ever leave? I cannot believe I'll still be practicing in the same place, in the same way, ten more years from now. I know I'm going to be back at the office next Monday morning. So sometime between Monday and ten years, I will probably leave. I think. Of course I didn't expect to be here this long already. And whenever I go, I know I will never forget this place, and will miss it profoundly.

A coyote has started yipping far off in the sagebrush hills; it has grown late and chilly. I must go to bed before my only neighbor out this way notices my light and comes over here in her bathrobe, alarmed, and certain that if I am up at this hour, someone must be terribly ill. . . . How could I ever forget this place: maddening and peaceful, frustrating and glorious, socially impinging and achingly lonely, alien and genuine, and home?

Life in the Slow Lane:
An Appalachian Experience

Murray Scher

SUMMARY. Murray Scher arrived in Greeneville, Tennessee, a very rural and traditional town during the heyday of the Sixties. He was unaware of the culture and depth of the Appalachian society into which he was moving to work as a psychologist. Slowly and painfully he navigated the demanding and intricate pathways of achieving a successful life and practice. This journey and attendant learnings, as well as errors and stumblings are outlined. The difficulties and benefits of working in this particular geographical and cultural setting for this practitioner, are enumerated.

During the past eighteen years I have often wondered why a nice Jewish boy from the Bronx was in rural Appalachia attempting to bring psychological services to the denizens of the bucolic hills. The answer invariably is: being challenged and being happy. There is a richness in rural small town existence which is absent in metropolitan, heavily populated areas. Of course there is much to gain in those places but the challenges and difficulties as well as the ease and support of small communities has been of great value to me in my own journey to personal and professional fulfillment. What I propose to do in this paper is explore how all of this came about.

When I emerged from the dynamic womb of graduate school in

Murray Scher, PhD, is involved in bringing psychological services to the green hills of bucolic East Tennessee. When not pursuing psychotherapy, writing, presenting, or consulting, he attempts self-renewal through running, swimming, collecting antiques, and being with his family. He has discovered that nurturance is very necessary for him and that he is primarily responsible for securing it. Toward this end he travels widely and spends altogether too much time on the telephone.

Requests for reprints should be addressed to Murray Scher, 905 1/2 Tusculum Boulevard, Greenville, TN 37743.

37

1971 the Sixties were still very much alive and the country was still in thrall to the liberal ferment of the times. My years in Texas had been startling in terms of my intellectual and emotional growth. Not only had I been ripe for the brainy stimulation of graduate work, but the tenor of the times had helped to raise my consciousness and to amplify my innocence.

Although my desire was to move west I could find no job and I decided not to accept a position at my University, thinking I would do better to leave the place of my awakening. So, I accepted a position at a small college in upper east Tennessee as a teacher of psychology half time, and as the counselor for the students the other half (the college's accreditation agency had demanded counseling services for the students). I thought it would be an adventure to go somewhere so backwoodsy. It was.

I think the innocence that was present in our culture plus my lack of awareness of what my limits were conditioned my decision. Interestingly enough, my wife did not accompany me to the interview, for two reasons: first we had a new baby and second, I never thought I would take the job. Also, although we felt ourselves to be quite liberated, in fact, we were not. We were still going to the place where I had the best opportunity despite the fact that it was she who had the more established career. Had she come with me for the interview, we would never have moved to Tennessee. She was more practical than I and would have seen what eluded me. The startlingly rural quality of the area and its denizens, the lack of sophistication, the lack of services, the inbred nature of the people, the narrowness of perspective, the overwhelmingly fundamentalist religious fervor of the natives, and the impulse toward maintaining everything just as is it was.

It might be helpful to have an understanding of who I am in order to place me in the context of my environment and my work. I grew up in New York City and am the product of the public school system including the Bronx High School of Science and the City College of New York. I then went on to Teachers College at Columbia University where I received a master's degree in Student Personnel Administration in Higher Education. After four years (two pre- and two post-master's) working in higher education I went to the University of Texas at Austin to pursue a PhD in counseling psychology. That was in 1968. I finished three years later and then as indicated headed to Greeneville, Tennessee.

This brief resumé does not tell much about who I am as a person so I think it valuable to add that I am a somewhat charming although reasonably compulsive perfectionist with a clear idea of not only how the world ought to look, but how everyone in it ought to behave. I am a liberal, non-sectarian type subscribing to all the basic liberated ways of viewing the world. I also spend too much money on antiques and too much time reading magazines. I like spy books and convoluted novels because they both inform me about psychotherapy. I also spend a good deal of time in physical exercise including running, swimming, and working out on muscle machines. I also attempt to externalize my creative urge by working extensively in my yard.

My training was typically end of sixties psychotherapy. A strong humanistic-experiential base with Rogerian and Gestalt approaches for the activity that I call therapy. My own therapy started out with a Freudian many years ago and for the last eight years I have seen (sometimes intermittently) a therapist analyzed by Harry Stack Sullivan. This therapist is an aged Chinese man who is much interested in Zen. He has had a significant impact upon me and upon how I do therapy, especially my current interest in working with dreams.

At one time I would have called myself "eclectic" but I prefer to use the term "independent" now, as the former sounds too dilettante-ish. How I function as a therapist is a product of who I am, how I was trained, what I have learned in therapy, and how I view the world. I am far more traditional and staid than once I was. I like to listen hard, respond empathically, introduce reason and humor, and to aid my clients on the remarkable journey of self-discovery of which we all are capable.

All the above is to help explicate what I expected when I first came to work in the green hills of Tennessee. I was naive and innocent although somewhat jaded. The latter a product of growing up in New York City and also needing to protect myself from the onslaughts of sophisticated friends and an overly optimistic, perhaps ridiculously optimistic family. The innocence was a product of the times, and the naiveté was a product of my ivory tower existence in academia.

I had a lot to learn from the local gentry, and they taught me a great deal. Some of what I was taught was based on my expectations. I came here expecting to have a great adventure. I thought I would be snug in a relaxed, somewhat backward environment to which I could bring enlightenment of a liberated and humanistic nature. I thought I could have a significant impact on the college at which I was teaching and would easily integrate into the community. Once integrated I would provide a useful and helpful understanding of human behavior and how to change it. This would of course speed the millennium bringing joy and fulfillment to all. I assumed that my wife and daughter and I would live happily in this kindly and enhancing environment and would flourish like Robert Young's family on "Father Knows Best." I also thought I would have time to write, travel, consult, do workshops, and generally continue what I saw as a promising professional career.

I was surprised at what met me and at what subsequently transpired. I got the first clue when my wife began screaming, "Where have you taken me?" when, from the main street of Greeneville, she observed cows. We had moved to a surprisingly rural and almost nineteenth-century area. A place H. L. Mencken had described as "the buckle on the Bible belt." There were thirty-five churches for a population of fourteen thousand in Greeneville, where I worked and we lived. The area was so far out of the mainstream that at the regional university in a nearby city where my wife worked she had to explain to them what the Hare Krishna movement was when a band of them showed up on campus dispensing cookies and beating drums. My students were a joy. Interested and naively worldly in a wonderful amalgam of sixties worldview tempered by life in the northeast as most of them came from there. They had a level of intensity and drive that was absent in the community.

East Tennessee was startlingly conservative for an area that was essentially very poor. It was overwhelmingly Republican and had been since before the Civil War or as it was usually called The War Between the States and actually once in my presence The Late Unpleasantness. There was no real tradition of charity except through one's church and the absence of social welfare programs as well as public services was startling. On the other hand the trust and kindness of the people was surprising. One's word was indeed one's bond and cars, refrigerators, and other major appliances appeared without down payments, deposits, or often signed contracts. I was alternately charmed and horrified.

The interstate highway system had not yet been completed through the area so it was a bit of a hassle to get here, but I found that rather nice and helpful in preserving the easygoing character of the region. I did not really miss the cultural events that urban dwellers proclaim as of excessive import to their happy existence. I began to learn about amateur productions and to see the value in them as well as the sometimes hidden artistry present. I was being introduced to a life I had only vaguely sensed existed. Forays into the country in pursuit of antiques and services provided a wonderful way of meeting people and viewing a world which to a great extent has disappeared in the relatively short time that I have lived here. I am not sure I miss it but I am happy to have seen it at such close quarters.

My feelings about the region and the way in which I live here and the impact of these on my work are of great importance. I think I would be a very different person and therapist had I lived elsewhere and practiced elsewhere. I do not think that I have necessarily absorbed the local worldview or mores and yet I am different. Perhaps it is just a process of aging but I think not. I am more accepting of many things. For example, I have always been skeptical to negative about religion, and that attitude has changed. I have learned how much comfort and guidance religion offers many of the people here and have found myself counseling people to talk with their clergy, join a church, become involved in one to which they already belong, and to seek solace in their faith. My beliefs and personal predilections have not changed but I have a much deeper and more humane view of the place of religion in the lives of other people. And I mean religion, not spirituality. The latter is an eighties concept that is not yet germane to Appalachia.

It has been a most pleasant experience to sit here in the mountains and watch the world rush by. Although this area has changed dramatically, I think the world in general has sped more rapidly along, but has not really advanced in ways that I find commendable nor enviable. Our social problems are far worse than they were twenty years ago and although there is a much larger segment of the population that is fiscally well off there is a also a much more disenfranchised and alienated segment of the population than ever in our history. In Appalachia I have observed the development of national trends in the rest of the country while living in a place that has escaped them to a large degree. This is not to suggest that we are not victim to many of the national problems but they do not seem as pressing here. It is true that social welfare programs are abysmal and that people are not well taken care of by the state and local governments, but the meanness seems to be from a poverty determined world view rather then from the greed that has motivated the federal government to abuse the populace. I am mentioning all of this as prelude to delineating how my position evolved and to make more understandable the way in which I practice in a rural area. My job at the college progressed reasonably and in due time I became tenured and advanced to the position of full professor. I became increasingly restless, and decided to open an independent practice that would provide some diversity and extra income. I did not believe that the area would support a full-time practice, as there were no others, nor did I really want one, as I felt secure in the bosom of academia. My happiness at the college deteriorated as the practice increased in size and after great soul searching (Scher, 1982) I resolved to leave the safe sinecure of the ivory tower and be my own employer. So I leapt. The decision was a wise and appropriate one.

I am able to maintain a private practice in a small town because I have lived here for a long time and have a good understanding of small town living and of the local populace. I am also able to do so, because I have evolved as a person and have changed sufficiently to deal with the vicissitudes of this kind of practice. A wife with a secure and lucrative job is also of inestimable help. However, the fright of independent work is not so much in the finances as it is in the violations of injunctions of the male gender role to work (hard) and to provide the bread for the family.

I think many of the personal issues involved in being in independent practice are the same no matter the geographical and demographic setting, but I also think that rural areas provide additional problems. There is usually lack of collegial support, there is a generally less sophisticated public, there is a sense of being out of the mainstream with few resources of a specialized kind for referral, and there is often the need to be a knowledgeable generalist. There is also difficulty in maintaining all ethical standards very strictly.

My practice is probably a bit unusual for a rural psychotherapist. I do not do any testing nor evaluations. I do almost no consultation. I do some professional development and a bit of supervision. For the most part my practice is individual psychotherapy and often of a long-term nature, although I do see a fair number of people for brief psychotherapy. I think my approach to my work is more a reflection of my own psychotherapy and the psychotherapeutic establishment in New York City than it is of my training or the world in which I matured as a therapist.

I believe that my practice is structured in this way because I did not know any better and also because I wanted it that way. As I am in many ways in a professional backwater I am away from the mainstream ideas and innovations except as I read about them in the professional literature or learn about them at professional meetings or through contacts with other therapists. Therefore, as I am a traditional person in many ways, and the area where I reside tends to be traditional if not reactionary, it was easy to stay in essentially the same path that I had originally entered when I went to therapy almost thirty years ago. It fits me, it fits the area, and it fits the people who come to me for therapy.

In recent times when more specific interventions are necessary, because of the proliferation of specialized approaches, and the emergence of specialized populations demanding to be treated in particular ways, I find there are more and more resources and I do make referrals to other professionals. However, as a good deal of my new clients come as referrals from former clients, they have a fairly good idea of what to expect and of what they want.

I have noticed, though, that I get a fair number of clients now from the Yellow Pages. That is a good sign as I think they are coming as a result of an increasing sophistication on the part of the local populace. When these people want to come for therapy they have no referral source, because going for therapy has been relatively rare so they turn to the telephone directory to find a therapist. This has advantages and disadvantages. I am glad of the increased interest and willingness to seek therapy. However, it is necessary to educate and indoctrinate these newcomers into the intricacies of being a client. They are remarkably willing and appreciative of my efforts. And I am grateful to them for their courage in entering into an unknown and potentially frightening enterprise.

I see mainly adults although I do work with children and adolescents. I find that sometimes I see several adolescents or several children concurrently. It is odd how it works out because often my practice is only adults and then suddenly a number of younger clients will show up. I welcome the change and enjoy the work, especially with the children. Adolescents, although often enjoyable to work with, are often very difficult clients.

When I left my college position to work in full-time practice I was struck with many of the differences in working with adults as opposed to college age adolescents. When I was trained I learned to believe that if the client was not cured in five to ten visits there was something wrong with me. That fit in perfectly with my natural inclination to be impatient. When I began to work almost exclusively with adults I discovered that it took a good deal longer for things to change for most people. That was a revelation and a delight. I began and have continued to enjoy long term psychotherapy and all that it entails.

My adult clients tend to come from the managerial professional class or segment of the local society. They are usually well-educated and somewhat sophisticated. However, as I have practiced over a longer period of time, I have seen many adults whose background and current status is lower class. Many of my physician referrals are people from this segment of society. The class of clients is not a good determiner of their presenting problem as most problems of adults cross class lines. I enjoy all the various kinds of adults whom I see. I respect their courage and resolution in seeking out and persevering in psychotherapy. I feel privileged that they choose me and stay with me. They enrich me in great measure.

I do see couples occasionally but am rarely satisfied with this endeavor. I am also not sure how much success I have in the maintenance of the marriage. I think the individual spouses often feel better after working with me but that does not guarantee that the marriage endures. Usually it does not. On rare occasions I see families even though I have always found that therapeutic morality to be satisfying.

The gender make-up of my practice was fairly consistent for a very long time but has of late begun to change. Usually sixty percent of my clientele was female and forty percent male, however, more recently the proportion is about fifty-fifty with even a slight edge to the male side. I am not sure the reason for this, but am pleased about it as my major professional interest has been on the effect of male gender roles in psychotherapy.

I have seen doctors and lawyers (but not Indian chiefs), bank presidents, captains of industry, corporate CEOs and accountants. I have probably seen representatives from every profession and many occupations. I have seen laborers and skilled craftspeople. I am beginning to see a fair number of therapists and that is a lovely compliment.

I think that the media has played a major role in the increasing sophistication of the general populace about psychotherapy as well as their acceptance of it as a good way to ameliorate personal problems. This has brought many people to me who would not otherwise have come. They are often wonderful to work with as they have come under their own steam and not through a forced referral. Their willingness to participate and the avidity with which they seek their own healing makes them a joy to be with and to assist. I am fortunate enough not to have many clients who are there under duress and, therefore, I do not have to deal too often with sullen and hostile clients. Often, when I do have such clients, they are adolescents and endemically sullen anyway. Alas, I do not enjoy that.

My clients have spanned most ages. The youngest I have ever seen was three-years-old and the oldest was eighty-three. The joy and wisdom at both ends of the age spectrum can be surprisingly similar although they are demonstrated in startlingly different ways. I have enjoyed the toddlers and the octogenarians as they are willing to share their secrets with me. The richness of every age has been shown to me and I must confess my wonder at the marvelous complexity of people and their experiences.

Northeast Tennessee, where I live and work has a very small multicultural population and therefore I have rarely seen anything but Caucasians. I have had black clients over the years but not many. That is a result of the socioeconomic status of the blacks here as well as of the paucity of their number. I have seen only one Oriental (an Indian) and no Hispanics or other minority groups. By far most of my clients have been native born but I have treated a few with foreign backgrounds.

The religious background of my clients has been almost uniformly Christian. I find that the denominations seem to go in cycles, although I am seeing a representative sample at all times. A kind of cluster phenomenon often occurs and I will find myself seeing a large number of Presbyterians or Episcopalians or as currently several Catholics. I have seen some Bahais and even a Moslem or two but never someone Jewish (my own affiliation).

There is a great similarity in the demographic qualities of my clients because of the costly nature of therapy and because of the lack of interest in it as a healing modality for large segments of the population. However, the homogeneity is more relevant to the qualities of the geographical area in which I work and what its history of population influx has been. There is diversity but it is not as great as in most heavily populated areas. The homogeneous quality of this area has caused me to cultivate professional relationships and activity in professional associations for stimulation and support.

I have a friend who insists that there is a direct correlation with time spent in a profession and size of telephone and air travel bills. My experience has demonstrated the accuracy of his belief. My travel agent loves me and likely so does the telephone company. All the people I know socially think that I am away as much as a traveling salesperson and there have been times when they were not far from wrong. I have participated actively in several organizations and have found the time and expense well worth it. When there was little to sustain me professionally at home, I could gain a great deal by attending meetings and talking with other professionals. I have always found that to be a deeply satisfying experience, and have received a great deal of support and encouragement.

When I returned from a professional meeting or workshop I was usually afire with ideas and enthusiasm. I felt a part of a vast network and no longer alone nor lonely as a professional. I was usually at my most productive. In recent years I find that when I get back from certain meetings I am razor sharp as a therapist and do some of my finest work. That feels wonderful.

I have used the friends that I have made through these excursions as consultants and as my network for support. I often call to ask questions about particular clients either if I wonder about how best to proceed therapeutically or if there is an ethical dilemma. I also cultivate as friends professionals who are unafraid of telling me when I am behaving inappropriately or am blind to my own involvement in the therapy of a client. Knowing that there are people out there who will deal with me honestly and fairly is a great source of encouragement to me as a professional. It is a kind of available safety net.

To ensure that I will be willing to use the safety net and not delude myself too badly, I have been in therapy on and off during the time that I have lived here. I have had to journey a considerable distance over the mountains for that therapy but it has been worth the effort. My therapist has helped me to be honest enough with myself that I have been willing, although sometimes reluctantly, to question my circle of consultants when I felt that I might not be doing the best job possible for my client.

I have been very fortunate in the people that I have befriended and been befriended by. They are usually dedicated and competent therapists or researchers in the field of psychotherapy and they have stimulated me greatly. I have been encouraged to think about therapy as a personal endeavor and as a philosophical/healing enterprise. This has helped me to work well with my clients and to achieve a deep satisfaction in what I am doing and how I perform as a therapist. This pondering about the therapeutic enterprise plus a drive to resolve a developmental crisis occurring at age thirty-five have combined to press me to write. My colleagues have both encouraged that enterprise and have at times joined me in it to my permanent joy and gratitude.

I have written elsewhere about the crisis that prompted me to write (Scher, 1982) and I have subsequently realized how very significant that decision was. The writing has provided an outlet for creative urges and productivity that is essential for me in this phase of my life. I think there is likely a push toward creating after we are beyond the childbirth and child rearing years of our lives. That may explain why so many people begin to garden or to cook or to do something that is creative or nurturing. I do all of those and so am getting in touch with how important the nurturance of life is for me.

My writing has also provided a way for dealing with the sometimes sterile professional atmosphere of the geographical area in which I work. In many ways I am a senior therapist here and therefore I do not receive a great deal of stimulation as a professional. I am also relatively isolated from other professionals because of the nature of private practice and because of my nature as a loner. Writing causes me to think about what I am doing and also forces me to consult other therapists and writers in order to explore my ideas and to gain their reactions to what I have written or to what I am contemplating writing.

On some occasions when I have co-authored an article I have found the task to be most rewarding, because I have been forced to evaluate my ideas and to adapt to the thoughts and world view of another person. That is essential to avoid the kind of professional autism that it is quite easy to develop in solo practice in a rural area. Like people who live alone I am mainly interested in my own ideas and my own view of how and why events occur; the forced interaction that writing together provides is a most useful antidote to that easily developed one-sided view of the world.

I did edit a book with three others and although that was a stretching experience as a writer it also provided another experience that it is important to note here and to mention again at a later point in this essay. The book involved a large number of authors and therefore a good deal of coordination which I undertook to supervise. It was a difficult and onerous task. My obsessive and compulsive nature made it even more taxing for me than it might have been to a more easy-going person. I was not aware of the connection at the time, but my practice declined considerably thus increasing the pressure on me. What I subsequently realized was that so much of my energy was going into the book that there was not enough for maintaining my practice. I will discuss later the relation of energy and practice, but suffice it to say now, although writing can provide the energy which can fuel a practice, I have learned that it can also sap the energy which maintains a practice. I realize I must strike an appropriate balance and not be blinded by my drive to produce lest I lose the fertile ground which nourishes my production.

I seriously doubt that practicing in a rural area requires any more or less attention to detail in terms of the logistics of organizing and maintaining an independent practice. I do think that the arrangements are different and that there are different issues and concerns in the manner one goes about doing things. I see four areas as being of concern: referrals, maintaining client load, running an office, and staying in the public eye.

Getting referrals is an important element in maintaining and establishing a practice. There are two broad categories of referral sources: professionals and former clients (I would include families and friends of those clients). In rural areas there is generally a managerial professional class of which psychotherapists are a part. It is also frequently from this group that the bulk of long-term clients will come. Maintaining a practice in a rural area often requires a fair number of such clients, at least it does so in my case. Therefore, the source of referrals and the source of clients often overlaps. I have been in the position on many occasions to have my referrers as my clients. This can produce ethical complications but need not do so. That will be considered subsequently.

In a rural area it is relatively easy to have one's reputation damaged by a misunderstanding or a simple foul-up. There is a physician who initially referred clients to me, but who quit doing so when I did not recognize him at a local cocktail lounge. My popularity with various physicians seems to wax and wane and I am unsure as to the reason for this erratic behavior. I struggle to make sure it does not occur but I am not always successful. I send letters of appreciation, and indicate it if their patient has decided to enter therapy with me. I also let them know when termination takes place. I am fairly scrupulous about not discussing the therapy with them unless they call and ask questions in such a manner that I can answer without violating a confidence. They usually accept this approach as long as they are not kept completely in the dark.

Physicians are my major professional referrers. I have not worked excessively hard to gain referrals as my experience has been that I did not need to. The ones who are sophisticated to the damages that can be sustained by a psyche are prone to refer after they have done what they can medically. In general, most of the clients sent to me turn out to be willing to continue in therapy. They are good to work with and usually benefit from therapy. The medical doctors are more sophisticated than they are often given credit for being.

My other major source of professional referrals is attorneys. The referrers are usually people I have seen or those who have made contact with clients and use me if one of their clients should appear to need therapy. This is not a tremendous source, but one that is relatively consistent and again provides clients who are a treat to work with.

Referral from former clients seem to be the best ones. I suspect that clients who refer people whom they know have a sense of who would benefit from therapy and from contact with me. They have an intuitive sense of appropriateness of being in therapy as well as who is well matched with me. It is a real compliment for me when a former client recommends me. I maintain this referral source by treating my clients well. My care and concern for them is genuine and they know it. That is sufficiently growth enhancing, so they are willing to share me with others.

I do not live in the town where the bulk of my practice takes place. This has turned out to be a boon as most people seem happy not to run into their "shrink" in social settings, the supermarket, or the locker room at the Y. I once went to a reception in celebration of a new anthem at the Episcopal church. I was surprised at how many former and current clients were congregants. Most were quite comfortable with my presence although some seemed quite unhappy about seeing me out of my accustomed venue. Being out of the mainstream of my clients' lives has been of some help to me. It has made me more comfortable and able to remain independent and aloof if I really want to.

Maintaining one's client load is very much related to referrals. This is not, fortunately, only referrals from other professionals, because for much of my career those have been few and far between. Worse, people whom the physicians or therapists had worked with and could not find a way to help often palmed that person off on me. It was not because my expertise was respected, but rather that it was likely I would be willing to see the person. As I indicated above, most of my excellent referrals were from former clients.

Maintenance of client load is also due, I believe, to the energy I have available for my work and also to the manner in which I am functioning as a person. I have come to believe that when I am somehow in "sync" with the cosmos and open to clients and working with them that they will come. When my energy is very low and I am too distracted from the essence of my work I think that is somehow communicated and clients do not show up on my doorstep. When I was working on a book I was so strung out with worry and compulsiveness that the number of people I was seeing plummeted, which of course increased my worry and perseverative behavior, and, in turn, had a negative impact on my work.

I learned from that experience to be aware of my energy level and to try to maintain what is necessary to keep my practice going. I try to stay centered and to project my interest and commitment to my work. I also place my work with clients first, and forego other commitments in order to work with them whenever they are willing. I work three days a week but in recent years have been willing to see clients on other days if they cannot make other arrangements. I have also decided, that if I cannot see all that want to see me during the hours I have scheduled, I will see them on other days. My commitment to keeping my practice going is paramount.

I have found it useful to make myself accessible by telephone. I inform clients that they can contact me whenever they wish and that I will respond. I do not charge for phone calls. I have had very few who have called, and when they do it is with good cause. Because I live in a culture that is committed to being nice, helpful, and friendly this accommodation via the telephone pleases my clients even though the vast majority of them would never call me. My availability and willingness to be of assistance is reassuring and heartening for them.

Practicing here is different from doing so in a big city and one must accommodate. For example, most of my clients cannot afford therapy on their own so I have to be willing to accept insurance payments and frequently wait for the insurance company to pay. Every once in a while that is a royal pain, but for the most part it is acceptable and it enables people to come and work with me. I cannot use an answering service because too many people know each other and the risks to the confidentiality of the relationship are too great. In order to maintain my client load I must be respectful of the local culture and willing to abide by its folkways and norms. Actually, that has not been a chore, it has been a most pleasing experience.

The office I have and the way it is furnished and used has also contributed to maintaining my practice. My presentation of self both in and out of that office have also had a positive effect. My office is in a small building that is centrally located but rather secluded. It is doll-like in character and rather charming. It is nonthreatening and quite inviting but is clearly not a space that is local. It is sufficiently foreign for most of my clients that they feel separated from their usual environment and set apart from what they generally know from their surroundings. This is helpful both for therapy and for them in regard to understanding what is going on in their lives and minds.

When I have attempted to understand how my clients see therapy I have drawn the usual blank that anyone would draw in trying to envision someone else's conceptualization of the world. I think most if not all of my clients see me as another doctor who will provide some panacea for their life. Some of them eventually realize that they are the source of their healing, and that I am a kind of midwife to that amelioration. Some of these also sense the almost mystical qualities inherent in much of the therapeutic enterprise. In all my years of practice only one client ever came because he wanted to learn more about himself. He did.

I have attempted to create a consulting room that will aid in the healing of those who come to see me. The room is spacious and softly lit. All the fabrics are plush and soft and tactilely attractive. There are lots of books and various knick-knacks that have been assembled out of gifts from clients, souvenirs of travel, or from some special occurrence in my life. There is a minimum of art work and all of it soothing. The furniture is antique country except for upholstered furniture which is contemporary. The ambience is relaxing and subtly regressive. There are toys for children and a huge teddy bear for everyone. The velvet covered sofa has soft, unattached cushions which people often cradle or clutch.

My second office is similar although its colors are less soothing but it is cozier and more personal as it is my study at home. Its seductiveness is in its luxurious and comfortable quality. People want to curl up with a good book or warm friends or a nice brandy in this room. It also encourages trust and contentment. Both offices are nonetheless businesslike.

The combination of the comfort, coziness, and welcoming of my offices is important in the success of my work. Clients are very much influenced by their surroundings and I attempt to provide a suitable environment to aid in the therapeutic endeavor and to encourage the healing that each person wishes to accomplish.

I have shared offices for some ten years with another psychologist who now does mainly consultation and personnel selection. That has been an excellent arrangement because our secretary gives the place a professional air, aside from handling all the phone calls and a lot of the detail work attendant on a private practice. Clients are, I think, reassured that this is an operation of some substance and with the potential for longevity. Most people need a sense of permanence and continuation that a well-established endeavor has to offer.

Working in the kind of rural and somewhat backward area I do it is necessary to have as much credibility as possible. My office helps provide some of that. Because I refuse to dress in a usual style I have to provide some sense of normality for my clients and my office does a good deal of that.

My usual attire albeit generally not outlandish, although I have been known to do that too, is certainly not typical of the local populace. I wear bright colors and generally European styled clothes. I also tend to be somewhat trendy and stylish. Clients have described my attire as anywhere from classy to rock-groupish. It is hard to ignore what I wear over an extended period of time. Few do. Ultimately almost all like the way I look although they find it unorthodox or unusual. My sense is that clients basically like that as it gives them some license to be different or even extreme if they would like to do that. Therapists have as a major part of their task to be permission givers and I also do that through my appearance and the environment with which I surround myself.

As I live in a traditional and rather conservative environment I walk a rather thin line between being individual and being too flamboyant. Eccentricity, I suspect, is tolerated while being too far from the norm would not be. As a "shrink" I have a certain amount of latitude which is not available to most other occupations save those in the arts. It is important that I not offend people but it is also important that I do not blend in so much that I lose my persona. The latter is more important to me than it might be to most people because of who I am, which is someone who hates the thought of not being noticed.

Staying public is an important task for those practicing in rural areas. It is easy for the populace to forget that there is a therapist in town. I have never been completely comfortable with speaking to civic and other groups although I have certainly done it. I have not pursued this avenue actively and when I have done it I have rarely gotten direct referrals. What I did accomplish was to keep my name and occupation visible. That usually eventually led to referrals, or so I assumed.

I have not labored very hard to stay public as that is not my style. Unusually as I might dress and thus draw attention to myself, I am quite a private person and reserved in many ways. I have attempted to keep whatever referral sources I have open through letters and lunches. I have mainly managed to stay in the public eye as much as I have through my clients and the referrals they make. That has worked fine for me and I have been reluctant to actively build the practice. I have been fortunate enough to get away with that simply trusting that competence will shine through and bring clients to me. So far I have been accurate.

One other source of staying public has been the social contacts that I have made and maintained. Because many of my clients come from a group similar to the one in which I socialize my being involved in various community projects and social events has helped people to know me and thus to refer others to me. In an area populated as mine is this has worked quite well. It has created some stilted interactions insofar as friends or social acquaintances sometimes become clients. However, most people deal with the situations exceptionally well with little or no discomfort.

As one would imagine work in a small town or rural area is not factored into some clauses of the ethical standards for psychologists. It is virtually impossible where one is the only therapist in private practice (and the only other alternative is the community mental health center) not to have for clients people whom one meets in other segments of life. Long before I knew about the concept of dual relationships I came to the conclusion that my obligation was to keep my clients as far from harm as possible. This also included any harm that I might inflict upon them. There is certainly the possibility of harm in dual relationships although more likely the possibility of damage is in not having a sufficiently good handle on the transference/countertransference to do an adequate job of therapy. In order to avoid that occurrence as much as possible I sought consultation with other therapists if necessary.

There are now more options for therapists to refer potential clients to and so I have less of a problem with dual relationships. However, it is not possible to avoid that in every circumstance. After all in a small town there are too many involved relationships to avoid it completely. Should I not see the local television repairman if he comes. Or worse, if I have seen him what do I do if my TV set goes on the blink?

More problematic than intricacies of this sort is the not unusual occurrence of seeing the various people in some sort of human drama. This includes old lovers, spouses, playmates, sweethearts, employers, supervisors, and others of current clients. Confidentiality makes it impossible to reveal information that would be of positive import if only I could tell. Once I was seeing two girlfriends of the same man at the same time. If I could have done a little revelation I would have been able to make the lives of all three a good deal happier. But alas, I could not.

These situations happen with some regularity and I must be very careful to remember what I know and from whom so as to make sure I do not reveal information or the fact that a certain person is or has been in therapy with me. I have been successful at this as I have never been accused of revealing a confidence nor of identifying a client. I am sure that had I slipped up my practice would have suffered a good deal. I must confess I have enjoyed these situations although they have been a source of some concern for me.

It is impossible to maintain the kind of anonymity that classical psychotherapy has enjoined therapists to pursue. I find myself stark naked at the local Y confronting clients, some of whom are similarly unattired. I am not sure what that does for transference or countertransference for that matter but it has occurred. I meet clients at social gatherings or in the supermarket or at antique shops. We generally smile and say hello and then pass on. I try to warn those new clients who I am likely to encounter elsewhere. They are usually surprised at my warning and they are probably right but I continue to do it nonetheless.

Upon occasion I have agreed to take social acquaintances or even friends on as clients. It has always worked out although I think I am a bit more uncomfortable with the situation than they are. As well as I can I have always monitored what I am doing and how they are doing in therapy to make sure that I am not transgressing any boundaries and that the therapy is as helpful as it might be.

Maintaining boundaries is the relevant issue in all these difficulties. If I am aware of the dangers in practice in a small town or rural area and actively work not to delude myself as to what I am doing and what I am getting myself into, then it is increasingly difficult to act in an unethical manner — that is in the spirit of the ethical standards as opposed to the letter of them. I do not particularly like a situational approach to ethics, but I am also aware that oftentimes environmental circumstances give us little choice other than to approach the world in that manner.

I do know that once I have seen someone for therapy they can never see me completely as they might have had they not been in therapy and for that matter I can never see them unbiasedly. This has created some difficulty but also some rather nice situations, as I share a kind of warmth and closeness to some former clients which I (and they) would not have had otherwise. Just as in life where there are no hard and fast rules I find in my approach to therapy there are no hard and fast rules other than not to satisfy my carnal and excessively narcissistic appetites at the expense of my clients.

In order to guarantee my steadfast concern for my clients as much as possible I have been in therapy during most of my tenure as a private practitioner. That has helped me to stay honest and clear about what I am doing. I think it essential for therapists to be in therapy, especially those who do not have easy and regular access to colleagues who can provide a perspective and help to keep the therapist honest. My therapy has been exceedingly helpful for me in terms of my own growth and for my work as a therapist in aiding me to uncover my blind spots as well as teaching me some new ways to approach and treat my clients.

Maintaining my personal resource has been difficult as it is for most if not all independent practitioners. We spend our working lives taking care of people; giving of ourselves and our skills. It is easy to lose sight of our own needs and how we can replenish our depleted energies. Aside from individual contact with colleagues, locally when possible and on the telephone when not immediately available, I spend a good deal of time at professional meetings where I can be restored. The American Academy of Psychotherapists has been the chief source of my restoration. Because it is an organization of psychotherapists there is an immediate contact with whatever the basic issues we all face happen to be. The replenishment that I experience with this group is extraordinary and well worth what I contribute to the other members in return.

My family as well as my non-professional interests are also major sources for keeping me whole and functioning at an optimal level. I find it nice to immerse myself in collecting antiques and dealing with all the people involved in that game. It is also nice to read involved novels and espionage books. I am also blessed with a spouse who is not a psychologist and so is generally not terribly interested in divining psyches although she is usually an available listener. My social circle is politely interested in my work as I am in theirs, but we rarely if ever discuss any of it. What a relief! I travel a good deal and find that soothing and restorative, especially trips to other countries and cultures. It is nice to be out of myself, and to have the opportunity to see myself from different perspectives.

I have often wondered how I have survived in a place such as this because it is so foreign from where I grew up. I think the answer is that it has seduced me by giving me what I really have needed which is a sense of belonging and of rootedness. Aside from collecting antiques I live in an antique house where I carefully preserve traces of the people who have lived here before me (as I also do when I have furniture restored, in fact I like chips and marks and indications of ownership.) I always return to East Tennessee, glad that I live here. I am nurtured by it and so it is not a question of survival but of flourishing—which I have done.

Is practicing here in a small town different from working in an urban area? I think so. There is less choice for the consumer and therefore less choice for the practitioner. That means I often have to stretch myself to deal with a clientele I might normally avoid. Because it is poor and rural it also means I have to deal with less sophisticated clients and with some that cannot pay immediately. This means I have to be more patient both with their understanding and their reimbursement. That has helped me as I tended to be rather impatient. I have also been forced to learn how to explain the intricacies of human behavior and the human psyche in ways that uneducated people could grasp. That has been great because the only way to learn is to teach. I have been forced to deal with people who are culturally a cosmos away from me, and in doing so I have gained a greater respect for the diversity and unity of human experience. It has also made me a kinder and more accepting person for which I am most grateful.

Soliciting clients is done in different ways in areas such as this. Certainly talking to civic, religious, and other groups is helpful but less so than just slowly building a referral network through doing good work and enduring in the community. Here there is a great deal of stock placed in commitment to the community and willingness to remain. Experience professionally and of the local ethos is valued, even by those who have moved here recently. It is a very traditional place and although the conservative quality that seems to accompany that often irritates me excessively it also appeals to me. Again it is my own need for rootedness and connectedness. That is of value it turns out as it is valued by my clients.

The slower pace and bucolic quality of the area also helps in that people are less frantic and frenetic for the most part and thus are better candidates for the longer term therapy which most adult difficulties require. There is a kind of incipient trust here too which I think is absent in most urban areas and that makes the job of the therapist easier and more likely to be successful. People are often scarred here, but they seem less battered and bruised than they often do in large urban areas and that makes a difference in working with them. This is certainly far from paradise, but it is easier and more humane than my observations and knowledge of more densely populated and sophisticated places demonstrate.

I have counted many of the ways I love it here and I guess in doing so have answered to a large extent the question why someone of my background is happy and productive in the green hills of Appalachia.

REFERENCE

Scher, M. (1982) A midlife transition for a therapist. *Voices, 18,* 21-26.

Small Town Practice of Psychotherapy: Ethical and Personal Dilemmas

Suzanne B. Sobel

SUMMARY. This article renews some ethical and personal dilemmas faced by professional psychologists practicing in small towns. Special concerns regarding staff and how they are different from those in larger communities are addressed along with the ethical problems they pose. A discussion of personal dilemmas posed by being a parent and a resident in the community is included and related to the dual relationship provision of the Ethical Principles of Psychologists.

As funding for community-based mental health centers has become less plentiful, psychologists have looked to new markets for their services. The adoption of mandatory mental health benefit laws and freedom of choice laws by many states has contributed to the increased market for psychological services as has the increased understanding by employers of how the availability of mental health services for their employees benefits job performance and can decrease unnecessary medical utilization by the employee and his/her family. Many practitioners have changed their focus of practice from public settings to independent practice settings as public dollars have shrunk and agencies have employed less expensive therapists in a way to stretch their few dollars. And, many of these have

Suzanne B. Sobel, PhD, is in full-time private practice in Satellite Beach, Florida. She is the President of the Parent Advisory Committee of Surfside Elementary School in Satellite Beach and has served as the Chair, Brevard County Commission on the Status of Women and President of APA's Division of Children, Youth and Families and Division of Psychotherapy.

Request for reprints should be addressed to Suzanne B. Sobel, PhD, 1680 Highway A1A, Suite 5, Satellite Beach, FL 32937.

61

opened offices in areas which have traditionally not had services, that is rural and small town areas. Practicing in these areas, however, brings up special ethical and professional issues for the psychotherapist and unique personal issues that one does not confront as often, if ever, when practicing in a large metropolitan area.

Being a psychotherapist in a small town setting is exciting and a challenge to one's personal and professional growth. Most of the doctoral training that one completes does not address the unique issues that the small town practitioner faces (Sobel, 1984). Psychotherapists, to be successful, must create systems within their own community within which they develop their practice and professional support networks and they must be willing to make compromises in professional standards and ethical guidelines to effectively establish themselves as members of the health professionals within the community where their practices are located. Some of these issues were addressed in an article that dealt with independent practice in child and adolescent psychotherapy in small communities (Sobel, 1984). It is the purpose of this article to discuss in more detail some of the ethical and personal issues that confront psychotherapists in small town practices that often requires therapists to rely upon their best logical, professional and ethical behavior, for sometimes one has to walk within the "gray" areas in order to be successful as a professional as well as an individual living within the community.

Different opportunities in small town practice have been elaborated by Enright (1989) and Cohen (1987). They discussed, as has Sobel (1984), the context of the community and some of the problems that one is confronted with. Small time practitioners may be called upon to treat situations which they may not feel totally competent to treat, but, realizing that alternate services are great distances away, may choose to do so in order to keep the patient functioning in the community with the support of other health and mental health professionals (Sobel, 1984). Practitioners must be alert to the political climate of their area as well as to the knowledge that they may not have the personal privacy that one might like. In a recent presentation at the 1988 American Psychological Association meeting, Enright and Elfant (Buie, 1988), discussed some of their loss of personal privacy and what they have done to deal with it. It is the purpose of this paper to look at the ethical issues that are involved in dual relationships that come up in small town practices. Some examples will be presented of real life situations that I have encountered that have led me to realize that while the Ethical Principles for Psychologists (APA, 1981) give us standards to meet, that some of these standards are unrealistic within the small town context. This does not mean that the small town practitioner has a license to practice in an unethical way. It means that sometimes the small town practitioner may have to develop ways to cope with situations in order to continue to live in his or her community as well as to practice there. Also, some of these issues do not come up as frequently if one is single or have no children. But, when families are involved, some of the issues of dual relationships cannot be avoided. The practitioner often is confronted with maintaining the confidentiality of his or her client that comes into the office versus allowing a family member to pursue his or her activities while maintaining some discomfort because a patient or their family is involved.

A short discussion of this is included in the chapter on dual relationships and conflicts of interest in the recent book by Keith-Spiegel and Koocher (1985). They recommend that one try to eliminate the dual relationship problems as much as possible and cite three examples. Keith-Spiegel and Koocher also discuss the hazard of referrals of "significant others" yet such referrals can be very commonplace when practicing in a small town. At times some of these referrals are the result of the hope by one of the significant others of using the same therapist to gain information about the other person. More often, however, I have found that such referrals are genuine and the individual feels comfortable coming in knowing that someone who was important in their life benefited from or currently were benefiting from the services that I could provide. But let me go forward and discuss some of the problems that have been encountered by myself, my secretarial staff, and my family.

STAFF PROBLEMS

When hiring secretarial staff, it is extremely important for them to understand what confidentiality means as well as to understand that their employer is liable for breaches of confidentiality that they make. In hiring I make sure that I explain to the prospective employee that they are not to acknowledge someone who comes into our office outside of the office unless the other person acknowledges them first and my secretary is to stay as aloof as possible to individuals that have come in so as not to in any way give the impression that their confidentiality would be compromised. Yet, this is an ideal standard which in reality is hard to maintain. Working close to where the individual lives increases the likelihood that neighbors, acquaintances, members of a religious congregation, schoolmates, etc., of coming into the office. Frequently some feel that they should have some special relationship as they know my secretary outside of the therapeutic setting. Let me share some of the issues that occurred with my secretaries over the years that have led me to develop ongoing discussions about confidentiality with my staff in order to ensure that it is maintained at the highest level possible.

One of the first situations to occur was when my secretary's husband, who was extremely active in the soccer league for children, was assigned a team of children which had three of my patients on it. My secretary came in saying that her husband had received a list of the team players and she noticed that these three children were on it. She felt that would create some difficulties for her as well as for her husband, without him knowing. She and I sat down and discussed what the concerns were and a major one was that there would be more of an interaction with her outside of the office that she felt would be difficult for her. While I could not do anything about the three children on the team and potential therapeutic problems it could cause, we could eliminate my secretary's problem by having her husband coach a different team. Which is what he ended up doing. I know that her husband never knew which one or ones of the boys on that list were our patients, but he did know that for some reason there was a conflict. We, therefore, protected the patients' confidentiality and minimized dual relationship problems for my secretary.

Another situation had to do with her daughter, who was in the Brownies. A phenomenon that I have found is that when a child patient learned that my secretary had a child that is in their grade, they had a tendency to try to seek them out as friends or seek a closeness to them. Needless to say this can be worked out in therapy but it also brings out other issues which have to be coped with in the everyday world. A patient was in the Brownie Troop with her daughter. For a holiday project, the troop members were required to work in pairs. Her daughter was an easygoing child who was kind to children who seemed to not have friends. The patient was an isolated girl and the patient selected my secretary's daughter to be the partner and her daughter did not object. The problem presented was that then my secretary had to interface with the mother of the girl outside of the office which made her somewhat uncomfortable. Much of this had to do with the personality of the mother. Again, we sat down and discussed the matter intensively and resolved that the best solution would be for the cooking project to be done at the other girl's house with my secretary providing the materials and allowing a minimum of contact of my secretary outside of the office with this child's mother. But then the next matter came up. It was her daughter's birthday and the question arose as to whether her daughter was going to invite this patient to her party. Needless to say by this time the little girl had let her daughter know that she saw me as a patient, which is a typical phenomenon that children will indicate that they go to a therapist without much thought to it. We discussed this and felt that if her daughter wanted this child at the party it would be alright. It turned out, as it was, that her daughter opted not to have her.

PERSONAL ISSUES

I have confronted situations, as have my secretaries, that have had to deal with neighbors and neighborhood situations. Frequently, neighbors of my secretary or myself call in for services. Sometimes it is very difficult to turn the individual down as there are relevant reasons for them seeking my services rather than someone else's because of my particular expertise and location. Yet, on a whole when I have felt that this is someone I have to see all the time because they live near by, I have tended to discourage them from seeing me and encouraged them to see someone else and in fact have helped that individual to find a therapist and explain to them about the discomfort I am feeling because of the dual relationship.

However, one time I caved in but established some guidelines which I believe were very beneficial. This had to do with a young adolescent who lived around the corner from me but whom I knew because I would see her riding her bike to school when I was walking my dog and she would often stop to chat. In fact, I did not know her parents until they called in for an appointment frantically, pleading with me to see her because she had had so much trouble in junior high school that year and had been to three therapists unsuccessfully. The situation was volatile and I reluctantly agreed to see the teenager with certain constraints including that I would help them get over the crisis but they would have to seek long term treatment with another therapist should it be advisable. This family respected my privacy and we were able to successfully deal with the problem and get the teenager back on the right track within eight sessions. To the best of my knowledge, it is now four years later and she is doing well.

Being visible in the community and part of the political process which all practitioners in small towns eventually become to some extent, I was appointed to a county advisory board by the Board of County Commission and then to a second board. Much to my dismay, the initial appointment almost involved me having to deal with a patient of mine who had also been nominated for that board. However, it turned out that she opted not to take the seat on the board. Had she not, I am not sure what I would have done except to discuss with her the issue of us both being on the board and most probably I would have resigned. This is consistent with the beliefs that Elfant (Buie, 1988) had reported about his social isolation. But, my appointment to another board placed me somewhat in an advisory position over a patient's position with the county government. While it was not a direct advisory role, there was some discomfort which we had to discuss.

There have been times when I have been invited to social gatherings where I knew a patient would be there. If it is a very large gathering of forty or more people, I am not worried. However, for a small dinner party I find it uncomfortable to be placed in a social relationship with someone I have to deal with professionally and I have found, as others have, that often this dilutes the efficacy of psychotherapy. Thus, I will decline a social invitation if it involves a small group where an active patient or a recently terminated patient is invited. However, someone who is a former patient who has successfully completed therapy I do not have as much concern about although by participating in a social gathering where they are present, I would probably be closing the door for them to return to therapy should they need it. I never, however, accept a social invitation by a patient of mine, either active or former.

An interesting issue came up when in October, 1987 I decided to leave my single life and adopt a six year old girl. The problems that it has presented regarding dual relationships for me are ones which we are never trained with in graduate school nor can the ethics code totally deal with. They are problems that small town practitioners have. Upon adopting her and placing her in school, the two children that befriended her were a young boy who had been a patient of mine and outstretched a very big hand to her in terms to her adjustment and another child whose brother and sister had both been into my office for assessment. She continued to want to know why I would not have the boy over who let her know that he had come to my office, and she did not fully understand about the girl whose siblings had been in. It was easier to discourage my daughter from inviting the boy over to play but it was more difficult for a girl to understand why you do not want a girl to play. Both were very nice children. I anguished over the issue of dual relationship and my own discomfort with having a different type of relationship with the parents than one within the therapeutic context. However, I realized that I could not get in the way of my daughter's friendships even if those sometimes made me uncomfortable. Thus, when the girl's mother called and asked if my daughter could come and visit them, I agreed and have subsequently had the girl over to my house yet never her brother or sister who had been in my office as patients. This is an ongoing problem where my daughter makes friends and it turns out that children are former patients or have siblings who are patients or whose parents have been in. I have drawn certain lines about my own privacy and my lack of social interaction with them while aware that my daughter has a right to friends so long as the friendship is not a therapeutic acting out on the part of the other child. In a small town one can never totally avoid this issue when one has a child.

And last, the issue of accepting gifts and favors. Keith-Spiegel and Koocher (1985) discussed this in their book. It is something which can make one very uncomfortable. Personally, I have never been offered a large gift, but I have been offered bags of citrus fruit from patients and have graciously accepted that as I have small tokens at the holiday times such as baked cookies or small boxes of chocolate. With certain children in my practice I have found that it is important to acknowledge their birthday by either having a small cupcake with a candle or taking them out for a sundae. These have been ongoing things that I have done. The impact is so positive that it is one that I believe is important.

Thus, let me conclude by saying that I have shared with you some problems that I have come up against in small town practice. If I read the Ethical Principles of Psychologists (APA, 1981), especially principle 6a, which deals with the issue of dual relationships, I can say that this principle is a good guideline but it is much more stringent than one can operate with in a small town. Enright (1989), Cohen (1987), and Hargrove (1986) would all agree. Rather, what one needs to do is establish good guidelines for oneself to keep you from making yourself vulnerable as well as not making your client vulnerable. At times it does become necessary to discuss some of the issues with your family even if they are young children. Young children are able to understand the idea of confidentiality when presented within the right context. It is also very important to realize that not only you but your family as well as your secretary and any other employee and their families all come under the issues of confidentiality in dual relationships. I have had an open atmosphere in my office where there is ongoing dialogue about these issues for frequently neighbors of my secretary come in, a fourth cousin came in, etc., for services. Without this, we could not run as ethical a practice as I do. I also do rely on colleagues to be able to discuss problems when I feel uncomfortable about some relationships and to see whether perhaps I have overstepped or have not created a sufficient boundary. The ethics chair of the Florida Psychological Association has been helpful as would be ethics chair of any psychological association.

In closing let me state that I love practicing where I do. I love being able to look at the ocean from my window. I love the people I treat and the work that I do and I find that what has happened since I started my practice almost nine years ago that the rapid growth of our area, now the sixth fastest growing area in the state of Florida, has made my work more exciting and innovative and has given me many challenges. The ethical dilemmas can not always easily be resolved. It is important to remember when practicing in small towns that strict adherence to the ethical codes of the American Psychological association cannot always be made. It does not mean that one practices in an unethical or unprofessional manner. But rather, one has to develop standards which are one step away but to make them known to others. This has involved a strong sensitivity to community norms, knowledge of the community agencies and abilities to join a team of other professionals and educators in trying to assist the growth of our future generations no matter the context.

REFERENCES

American Psychological Association (1981). Ethical principles of psychologists. *American Psychologist, 36,* 633-638.
Buie, James (1988). Small town practice: Living in a fish bowl. *APA Monitor, 19(10),* 25.
Cohen, Dotti (1987). Rural area private practice. *Psychotherapy in Private Practice, 5,* 41-52.
Enright, Michael F. (1989). Small town independent practice: New Opportunities. Unpublished manuscript.
Hargrove, David S. (1986). Ethical Issues in rural mental health practice. *Professional Psychology: Research and Practice, 17,* 20-23.
Kieth-Spiegel and Koocher. (1985). *Ethics in Psychology,* New York, Random House.
Sobel, Suzanne B. (1984). Independent practice in child and adolescent psychotherapy in small communities: Personal, professional and ethical issues. *Psychotherapy, 21,* 110-117.

Anecdotes and Personal Reflections About Psychotherapy in a Rural Area

Adrianne C. Kadushin
Lewis R. Kadushin

SUMMARY. A wife and husband psychotherapy partnership will narratively describe their lives' work on the rural Eastern Shore of Maryland. In 1990 they will celebrate the 25th anniversary of their marital partnership and 18 years of a professional partnership. They still feel they have a great deal to offer each other and to the many folks who avail themselves of their varied caring and supportive services. Their perception is that the key to successful living is through healthy relatedness and relationships. The following paper will attempt to highlight the components of their gratifying and fulfilling private practice.

HISTORICAL DEVELOPMENT OF OUR PSYCHOTHERAPY PRACTICE

1960 – 1972

Two New York City kids, born and raised in the Big Apple, grow up, meet and begin developing a relationship during their late teens

Adrianne C. Kadushin, MA, RN, CS, is a certified clinical specialist in adult psychiatric and mental health nursing. She is certified by AAMFT (American Association of Marriage and Family Therapies), AASECT (American Association of Sex Educators, Counselors and Therapists), ASPO (American Society for Psychoprophylaxis in Obstetrics Inc.), NBCC (National Board of Certified Counselors) and ANA (American Nurses' Association).

Lewis R. Kadushin, PhD, is a licensed psychologist, certified by the Maryland State Board of Examiners of Psychologists, a member of APA (American Psychological Association), and MPA (Maryland Psychological Association).

The couple is in a conjoint psychotherapy private practice. Request for reprints should be addressed to Psychological Associates, 206 Kay Avenue, Salisbury, MD 21801.

and early twenties. Both are moving gradually toward careers and interests in the health sciences. The girl becomes a licensed registered nurse, providing the initial support for both to continue working toward advanced degrees which ultimately lead to careers in the mental health field. They eventually marry and leave N.Y.C. in 1968, spending three years in Texas, one year in Florida and finally settle down in 1972 in the rural city of Salisbury, Maryland, with a city population of 16,000 and a county population of 50,000 people. Located on the Maryland Eastern Shore, Salisbury is a regional hub of the rural Delmarva Peninsula, famous for Maryland Blue Crab and Perdue Chicken. In the early '70s it was hardly a sophisticated community and mental health services were minimally available and very suspect.

1972 – 1979

There were several things about us as a professional couple that helped put us "on the map" and provided us the public relations and name recognition needed to establish a reputation that eventually resulted in a very active full time joint psychotherapy practice. Initially we came to the Eastern Shore at the invitation of the University of Maryland Eastern Shore, formerly Maryland State College. University of Maryland had recently incorporated the Eastern Shore campus into its statewide system; it is located in Princess Anne, a town twelve miles south of Salisbury with a population of about 1200. The campus had no psychological services and my husband, Lewis was hired as a psychologist to provide the first psychological services and to begin a modest counseling center. Just prior to the move from Miami, Florida to Salisbury, Maryland our daughter was born. During the pregnancy I took action on a long term interest in primary mental health prevention by training and becoming certified by the American Society for Psychoprophylaxis in Obstetrics, Inc. as a Lamaze childbirth and parent educator.

Soon after our arrival in Salisbury with a nine month old baby, I discovered that I was in great demand as a childbirth educator by a core of sophisticated pregnant couples seeking family centered maternity care. Up to that point, Lamaze childbirth including preparation of a father or significant other to accompany mother in labor and delivery, did not exist on the Delmarva Peninsula (a geographic region comprising a portion of rural Delaware, Maryland and Virginia). What I had to offer was viewed as radical by a very conservative medical community. For Lewis and me that presented an exciting challenge. We decided to team up as a husband and wife Lamaze teaching team, a strategy rarely implemented as a teaching method throughout the country at that time. Our charismatic humanistic client-centered orientation and teaching style proved to be instantly successful. Never mind that we were the only "game" in town. We became childbirth education gurus with many devout followers as well as some enemies amongst the medical community. What we were not was unknown. In a small community, we received a lot of publicity and people turned to us for information, advice and support on everything from breastfeeding, care of sick children, family planning and the mid '70s meat boycott. Our views on controversial issues were constantly sought and we were interviewed by local newspapers, television and radio stations.

All of the above provided us with notoriety which helped support our growing private psychotherapy practice. While Lew was employed at the university, for the first six-and-one half years, I began practicing with another psychotherapist in private practice. In addition, Lew and I started our own part-time practice in the early '70s. During those early years, I became certified by the American Association of Marriage and Family Therapists (AAMFT), American Association of Sex Educators, Counselors and Therapists (AASECT), and more recently the National Board of Certified Counselors (NBCC). We had completed our highest academic degrees prior to our arrival in Salisbury. I received my MA degree from New York University in 1968 and during the same year Lew received an MEd degree from Columbia University. In 1972 he completed a PhD at University of Texas in Austin.

In the early '70s, as psychotherapists in a rural community, we were looked on as being New York City Jewish upstart intellectuals who were part of the hippy fringe relocating to an area for the purpose of imposing our counter-culture views on an innocent naive populous already satisfied and content with services rendered by the medical community. We waited six-and-one-half years to announce the opening of a full-time private practice and meanwhile we never turned down a speaking engagement. One day we received a request from the local medical society to discuss assessment, diagnosis, and treatment of sexual dysfunctions. That request may be the most memorable because the medical community was comprised of some of our most formidable adversaries. Their attitude until that time was that they never saw a sexual dysfunction that could not be cured with medication or just ignored. At last we were being acknowledged as possessing some credibility. Soon after we began receiving medical referrals. Twelve years later we are receiving referrals from medical doctors for a wide variety of disorders. Concern for the lethality of such conditions as hypertension, eating disorders, anxiety attacks and panic disorders has led to a growing awareness and respect for the services of psychotherapists and increasingly we feel a growing trust from the medical community. They have come to realize that for the benefit of the patient, a multidisciplinary approach is required. We, in turn, make ourselves available to answer questions from referral sources concerning our services.

FACTORS AFFECTING THE EVOLUTION OF OUR PRACTICE TO ITS PRESENT FORM

1979—

In 1979 Lewis resigned his university position and we turned our part-time private practice into a full-time one conducted in our home. We have maintained financial independence from the very beginning, maintaining a highly visible profile by being versatile and available in many ways in the community. Shortly after Lewis left the university, a community college was founded in Salisbury. Since its inception, he has taught introductory psychology and human relations courses every semester. His students represent a broad spectrum of the community with many older students in the fields of law enforcement nursing, business, drug and alcohol counseling, hotel/motel management, tourism, real estate, child care and education. Both of us enjoy public speaking and having come out of the growth group movement of the '60s, we are always willing to set up workshops and seminars for interested groups in our own city as well as surrounding towns and those two adjacent states. Many of our public speaking engagements are offered as a public service to the community. In a rural area, where organizations operate on meager budgets, often they are unable to pay a speaker's fee. Instead we might receive a gift. Recently I came home with a fruit basket after speaking to a chapter of T.O.P.S. (Taking Off Pounds Sensibly). What is more important than any fee is the good will built by being available to groups of people who themselves provide a valuable service to the community.

"Girls Are Great," the title of a girl scout project selected by fifteen third grade girls in a local troop as their winter activity, is the topic I focused on recently at the request of the troop leader. I was enthusiastic about the opportunity to focus on the self-esteem of a future generation of young women, seeing it as another aspect of my work in enhancing mental health. While on the phone with the troop leader, as with other requests for our public speaking services, I inquired about how she located our agency. In this case, she had looked to the county Board of Education as a source of referral information and discovered a listing of helping agencies. Psychological Associates, the official name of our partnership, was on the list. Several years ago I had served on one of their advisory boards examining guidance and counseling provisions in the public schools. More recently, we have had regular contact with many of the school guidance providers through involvement with the local chapter of the Personnel and Guidance Association. Building a successful private practice in a rural community requires the concurrent willingness to focus on building good will by reaching out to folks who sense and intuit the value of psychological services for prevention and education.

In addition to childbirth education, we are on contract with a local independent school where we teach a sex education program for seventh graders, entitled: "Human Development: Responsibility and Decision-making." We began the program in the early '80s while our daughter was attending the school and her class was used for the initial pilot study.

We have a deep and abiding interest in the prevention of child physical and sexual abuse. Each year I teach several parent education series that are sponsored by a county youth and family service agency. Lewis provides clinical supervision to the staff of the same agency and psychological testing for the clients who require it. Over the years we have also provided service and support to the tri-county life crisis agency whose focus of attention is primarily women and child victims of violence as well as providing a twenty-four hour a day telephone hotline.

To keep current educationally and clinically, and to maintain contact and open communication with colleagues, we sponsor, support and/or participate in local continuing education workshops and provide support and supervision to mental health professionals who request our services. We must travel a minimum of three hours to reach Washington, Baltimore, or Philadelphia for most of our own continuing education.

We affirm the work of other colleagues and agencies, not feeling threatened because we know that it actually enhances us to have more and better competition to increase the level of community awareness and acceptance of mental health services and to keep us "on our toes." We have developed excellent rapport with family practitioners, some of whom have taken a more caring and empathic interest in our clients than our psychiatric community who view us as competitors. Over the years, as new and additional mental health providers have joined the provider pool, our own practice has grown. Even the uniqueness of our husband/wife therapy-teaching-consulting team has been challenged, but we are flattered rather than threatened because we know it stems from the popularity of our services and that we are role models for healthy personal and professional relatedness as a marital couple. Not wanting to seem arrogant, I believe that in an age where everything including marriage seems to rapidly depreciate and be easier to dispose of and replace than work on and repair, we serve as an inspiration to those who want to maintain their relationships, understanding that they are what makes life most worth living. I suppose you could say that we genuinely believe in what we preach.

Our professional practice has been home based from its inception. Residential zoning codes became an issue and temporary obstacle when we formally announced the change to full-time status in 1979. To avoid legal conflicts and hassles with those who were still threatened by us, we literally moved around the corner to a second home which was zoned partially residential and partially commercial and gave us freedom to operate without anyone threatening to close us down using zoning code violations as a weapon. Prior to purchasing the home, the attached double car garage had been converted to a two bedroom wing with full bath, foyer, lots of closet space and a door to close off and separate the wing from the rest of the home. We now use that wing for our office/therapy rooms exclusively. Many clients comment on the comfortable ambience including a level of privacy and anonymity provided by coming to a home office. To their way of thinking, should someone notice their car in our driveway, it might be there for many reasons, only one of which includes being involved in psychotherapy. Eventually, worry of "being discovered" fades from the foreground of clients' concerns once they realize that to be in therapy does not place them in the category of crazy or inferior. Initially, however, it's of paramount concern.

Practicing psychotherapy in a small town definitely requires creativity and flexibility because we do interface with clients in many social and community settings. However, we don't view that fact as an obstacle but rather as a workable and often useful parameter to negotiate and come to grips with. Sometimes personal aspects of relationships are set aside temporarily for weeks, months or years, sometimes forever. Our priority is to be therapeutic to those who need us.

We are located on a street that is partially residential and wooded and then becomes commercial as it intersects with the main north/south highway running the length of the city. It is a convenient location for our clients as well as being a practical, convenient arrangement for us, maximizing our own privacy. We love the flexibility of working in our home and being able to arrange our schedule to meet the various needs of clients for early morning and late evening sessions and yet being able to use hours in-between to meet a variety of professional and personal needs. Each day is interesting, different, and can be rearranged to accommodate last minute unforeseen activities and responsibilities. This was particularly valuable when our only child was living at home. Today she is seventeen and a high school senior attending a boarding school in New Jersey. She always appreciated our availability and constant physical presence. When she arrived home from school, one of us was always home to greet her. We felt relaxed and comfortable as parents knowing that our careers were not preventing us from doing the most important mental health job of all, attempting to raise a healthy human being.

THE PHILOSOPHICAL AND THEORETICAL BASIS OF OUR PRACTICE

During the early years of our practice most of our clients held unrealistic expectations of psychotherapy. They were familiar with models of intervention which required them to be passive recipients of expert advice and, therefore, not being responsible for the change process themselves. In order to orient clients to be active participants in the therapy process we found it necessary to describe the responsibilities of therapist and client and the process itself. Today a larger percentage of new clients understand what they are getting into but we still rarely take that understanding for granted.

We tell clients that our responsibility is to establish and maintain a special environment that would maximize the likelihood of "healing" for the client. We discuss issues such as confidentiality, unconditional positive regard, and other ingredients that create a caring and safe environment in which clients can confront themselves to learn who they are, how they got to be that way and accept that they are ultimately responsible for their behavior. In a rural area comfort within the therapist/client relationship is determined foremost by level of trust in the confidentiality factor.

It is our belief that most human beings possess a healing force which enables them to form better and better "gestalts." This psychological healing force is similar to the physiological healing force that operates best when we create the conditions that foster healing. If we cut our finger, a miraculous process takes place; the tissue will knit itself closed and if we care for the wound by keeping it clean and bandaged then healing will be faster and more complete. The special environment we create enhances the psychological healing force, giving it a chance to operate for the client. This process empowers the client to use the improving "gestalts" to effect change in her/his life by either taking action or changing cognitive structures that lead to a greater sense of wellbeing. A client may realize that she/he does have the power to make choices and cope with the consequences.

By discussing what the therapy process is and what assumptions we make about healing, our rural clients are enabled to make better use of their therapy. It is one of the ways we have discovered that encourages spontaneity so that the therapy process is then based on the client's own momentum and will to move, rather than being pulled in directions which are the therapist's. We see our responsibility as being one of using our skills of observation, awareness and ability to develop rapport and relatedness so that we are available when spontaneous moments of potential growth and healing appear in the therapeutic relationship. When the therapist/client relationship facilitates such junctures, people seem to move effortlessly toward a more positive way of relating to self and others.

An eclectic, psychodynamic, cognitive, behavioral, family systems approach is required for the diverse type of practice we have developed. We are generalists with a family practitioner-style mental health practice. The formal part of our education may have ended years ago, but we study and research regularly to meet the challenge of special needs presented to us by each developmental crisis and stage of the life cycle that crosses our threshold. What this does for us in return is to help us avoid burnout. We are constantly stimulated and challenged, rarely bored and stale, because we avoid specializing in one specific diagnosis or type of problem and also avoid just one psychotherapeutic technique. The variety of our client base demands creativity and flexibility.

We have discovered a direct relationship between our trust of clients and their ability to eventually orient themselves toward a healthier life direction and the degree to which they will cooperate with recommendations made by ourselves and other caregivers. Let me underscore that we trust the people we are working with, believing that the psychotherapeutic process is most importantly a respectful affirming relationship. Those clients who take advantage of that affirmation and trust, begin to trust themselves and eventually discover the tools to heal themselves. We respect attempts to use many alternative healing approaches, as long as they promote a reflective and flexible attitude toward oneself, one's body and emotional and social life. "Going with the flow," PMA/positive mental attitude, "Nam-Myoho-Renge-Kyo" (Buddhist chant), imagery and visualization, relaxation techniques, mantras and meditation, are only some of the self-help theories, methods and tools used in conjunction with therapy by many of our clients. The longer we remain in the field of psychotherapy the easier it becomes to respect each person's unique search for a truth that heals. What makes it increasingly easy is our growing humbleness and admiration for those persons with courage enough to continue the journey and life long search for a truth that is never absolute.

Networking with practitioners from many disciplines we consider to be part of our professional responsibility and it helps us provide broader based service to our clients. We frequently refer clients to other resources. We spend time getting to know new members of the professional community and investigate how their services might supplement our own, providing additional services beneficial for the people we serve. Valuing our own privacy and requiring the utmost of confidentiality for our client population, we have never employed an in-house secretary, office manager or bookkeeper. We utilize a telephone answering machine and as an extrovert I (Adrianne) rarely mind answering the telephone and returning messages. What that affords us is the ability for new and old clients to talk directly with therapists and in that process we may provide networking services without ever seeing the caller. So many of our mental health service providers and agencies are located in a small concentrated area serving a wide geographic region, making it convenient for us to "drop in" for a cup of coffee and an informal "getting to know you" chat. Bureaucracies are less cumbersome in a rural area and usually we can have clients seen without excessive delay.

DURING A TYPICAL DAY . . .

It's a Tuesday evening, 9:30 p.m. I have just returned from the town of Berlin located about twenty-five miles from Salisbury. T.O.P.S. (Take Off Pounds Sensibly) has a chapter in Berlin and for the second consecutive year the membership has requested that I present a program. Tonight I was accompanied by a client of mine who weighs 375 lbs. and has struggled with obesity all of his life. He accepted my invitation to join me in speaking to the group about his personal struggles. He had never spoken in front of a group and it took tremendous courage to do so this evening. The most exciting outcome of tonight's experience is that my client has decided to become a member of the T.O.P.S support group, something he has wanted to do for quite some time . . .

Earlier today I saw a 16 year old boy and his family. The boy's friend, age 13, killed himself in his parents' bedroom three days ago using a rifle he had received as a Christmas present. The client felt he might have been partially responsible for his friend's suicide and was experiencing depression . . .

During the same day Lewis sees a 47 year old mother of four children who reported that her husband (second marriage) is physically and sexually abusing her. She grew up in an abusive environment and had twice married violent men. Along with individual therapy, he recommends she join a support group of battered spouses sponsored by the Life Crisis Center . . .

A 31-year-old single male, realizing success as a professional business manager, comes to see Lewis complaining of inability to cope with the failure of a relationship with a woman. He has suffered from depression since adolescence and has a variety of erroneous beliefs about himself and the world that leaves him powerless to act in his own behalf . . .

Upon returning from this evening's speaking engagement, there's a message on my answering machine from the Dean of Students of a private independent day school in the Delmarva area. There's been an episode involving the abuse of drugs and alcohol by some of the high school students. Disciplinary action has been taken and he feels the students need an opportunity to speak with a professional counselor as a group. This kind of request is one of my favorites; we set a date and for this experience we arrange for my daughter to participate and help facilitate the student dialogue . . .

I am amazed when urban colleagues talk of specialty practices where only certain diagnoses are seen and all other cases are referred to other specialists. I suppose that nowadays it might be possible to specialize only in sexual dysfunctions, for instance, but certainly that would not have been possible in the early years of our practice. The reality of rural practice forced us to become generalists and neither of us has regretted that decision. My favorite expression is "I'm never bored" and I've not yet experienced burnout.

The diversity of our practice helps us avoid burnout. It is also easier to avoid burnout if you're vigilant about maintaining balance in your life. We do that by viewing our personal life and space as equally sacred and important with our professional life. We try to adhere to a four-day work week so we have time to play, rest and get away from the scrutiny of the public eye or magnifying lens/fish bowl life of small town living. We maintain relationships with friends in cities along the eastern seaboard and across the country. Traveling is a therapeutic oasis for us. We have a customized van and we're on the road often. This coming weekend we will be heading to the North Carolina beaches.

WHAT DO WE WANT TO DO WHEN WE GROW UP?
MORE OF THE SAME

Lewis and I are forty-nine and forty-six respectively. Having practiced in the same region for the greater part of two decades, we derive the additional satisfaction of meeting and providing service to several generations of the same families. Over the years we have witnessed an enlightened trend in the general population with growing respect and appreciation for what psychotherapy can offer in terms of health maintenance and prevention. We were far more suspect and appeared to many as subversive agents in the 1970s. The remoteness of the geographic region tends to keep the area about a decade behind in awareness and adoption of new trends of thinking. There's a certain charm and quaintness to that reality if you come to accept and appreciate the slower pace of life that is the outcome of geographic isolation. And as Lewis and I age, our patience and tolerance grow, leading to a healthy respect for the advantage of "going with the flow."

Almost two decades ago, intuition helped us conclude that after twenty-five years of big city living, there might be an advantage if we were willing to risk a major shift from urban to rural living. Having extensively experienced both lifestyles, we know there is a price to be paid for either choice. We have been little fish in a big pond and currently are bigger fish in a small pond. When there are fewer professional resources there is certainly less competition but also greater professional isolation. Our professional membership affiliations provide opportunities for coming together in order to learn and share with each other. But geographically we are several hours away from the majority of usual meeting places. On the other hand, we have been able to lure special interest speakers and professional workshop facilitators to an area renowned for its recreation and leisure opportunities. We attend out of town conferences at least three to four times a year. Ultimately I believe it is equally possible to develop a successful private practice in urban and rural areas. However, it was the limited number of agency and organization positions available in a rural setting that gave us greater impetus to begin a full-time practice — a venture we might not have risked if we had remained in urban areas where employment opportunities were more substantial and diversified. We chose Salisbury and the rural Maryland Eastern Shore because we wanted to get away from the urban rat race. Salisbury has the cultural and educational opportunities, low taxes and environment conducive to living as if we were semi-retired but still being very productive. It is a regional hub of activity but without the expense, pressure and traffic jams of Washington D.C. We can commute from here to D.C. in thirty-five minutes by air (from the regional airport) or two-and-one-half hours by car.

Writing this chapter in 1989 has made us even more aware of the decade we will soon be concluding and how it has impacted on our views of rural psychotherapy practice. What we have seen in the 1980s is that time has become a more precious commodity than money. Households with two adults working outside the home, leaving no one to provide nurture, care and maintenance, many single family households, the explosion of technology requiring all of us to race to keep up, remain current and accumulate ever-increasing quantities of information, all this leads to a frantic pace of life with no time to stop and "smell the roses." Our rural area is not immune to the '80s phenomena but the rat race is not nearly as frenetic as it is in urban settings. Moreover, by the late '70s we had inaugurated our version of a cottage industry, developing our private practice and in a home setting as well. Having been raised in New York City and seeing the wear and tear on our parents who had to endure long daily commutes to work, we knew it was an absolute bottom line requirement that we not have to travel long distances to work. A home office certainly ensured that requirement.

Our overwhelming conclusion is that these two N.Y.C. kids made the right decision when we decided to make a drastic change and explore rural opportunities. Yet there have been disadvantages, as there are in choosing any option. And just as we have encouraged the development of flexibility and adaptability in our clients, we have encouraged ourselves to develop similar skills and a positive orientation toward life. As a result, advantages of rural practice and life style have been maximized for us and disadvantages seem easy to manage and work around. It has been a pleasure to prepare this chapter, giving us a chance to share with fellow professionals in the mental health discipline, the joys of our particular lifestyle. Actually our only slight concern is that our story will sound so inviting that we will soon be inundated with professionals wanting to escape urban living!

Ethics of Rural Practice

Floyd L. Jennings

SUMMARY. Special ethical problems are posed by the practice of psychology in rural settings. The nature of rural values, bonds to land, relationships created by contiguity rather than intentionality, and lack of anonymity, all contribute toward creation of special problems with dual relationships for the practitioner. Ordinary prohibitions against dual relationships may be excessively inflexible and deprive patients of treatment without opportunity for accessible alternatives. The practitioner must exercise both special sensitivity and special attentiveness to ethical issues. Several cases are discussed.

INTRODUCTION

The practice of psychology in rural areas poses a host of problems, yet presents a plethora of delightful possibilities—few of which will be discussed in this article, but remain carefully preserved secrets for those who seek out a slower and quieter pace of

A current resident of Houston, Texas, Floyd L. Jennings, PhD, has practiced in both rural and urban settings. While now in private practice and Adjunct Assistant Professor of Psychiatry and Behavioral Science at the University of Texas Medical School, he was one time Director of Mental Health Programs for the Indian Health Service, Santa Fe, New Mexico. In the 1970's he started a community mental health center in Worland, a community in northern Wyoming, near the home of his youth.

Dr. Jennings is a graduate of The University of Texas Southwestern Medical School (PhD, 1972); Southern Methodist University (STM, 1979; BD, 1964); and McMurry College (BA, 1961). He is a member of APA, past president of a Bell County Psychological Association in Texas, a fellow of the American Group Psychotherapy Association, and past-president of both Southwestern and Houston Group Psychotherapy Societies.

Requests for reprints should be addressed to: Floyd L. Jennings, 7777 SW Freeway # 1036, Houston, TX 77074.

85

life, who find great pleasure in actually knowing their neighbors, in solving their own plumbing or mechanical problems, in savoring the crispness of a winter's morning when the snow lies soft and quiet on the landscape and there is neither pollution by noise of vehicular traffic nor fouled air.

The following comments will focus upon ethical issues as may be presented in a singular fashion to rural practitioners, including reflections about the development of standards of practice in general, and special problems associated with dual agency, or dual relationships in rural practice — problems which require an equally special resolution, a resolution which may be somewhat at variance with standards in other settings.

THE DEVELOPMENT OF ETHICAL STANDARDS

It is axiomatic that all social structures develop standards of behavior and/or conduct. Professions — insofar as they represent a social structure — exhibit behavior common to other social structures; that is, professions go through a developmental cycle such that with increasing maturation and differentiation, there is increasing specificity as well as complexity with regard to training, rites of passage into the profession, and behavior expected of the professional.

Indeed, though such a charge might be regarded as excessively philosophic (and/or theological), ethicists within professions — just as professional ethicists — reflect upon good and evil, and it is only with some commonly accepted cultural notions of what constitutes good, that ethical principles are derived. Such principles are not derived with the clarity of Aristotle's *Ethics* but are commonly accepted with many unstated presuppositions. Professional prohibitions focus more upon undesirable behavior than articulation of what might require the judgment that said behavior is undesirable; e.g., articulation of *why* it is "evil" for a professional to have sexual relationships with his or her patients.

The logical reasoning which underlies ethical prohibitions are generally unarticulated, but commonly accepted, i.e., that sexual relationships are undesirable because such relationships between doctor and patient are examples of multiple categories or types of relationships, dual relationships, if you will.

Dual relationships are ones in which behaviors may occur that are proper in one context but not necessarily proper in another. (Note the use of "value" words such as "proper" — words which are themselves unexamined as beyond the purview of professional casuistry, but which reflect some perception of goodness as well as evil.) Sexual behavior is deemed proper in an interpersonal context truly involving mutual consent, and in some quarters, commitment to the endurance of that relationship. Professional relationships carry a set of unstated, but felt, conditions, or warrants, with which sexual intimacy is inconsistent. One such warrant has to do with equity in a relationship as a pre-condition for sexual intimacy. Professional relationships are not relationships of equity — though deep respect of the other's personhood is generally seen as a precondition of positive outcome in treatment. Professional relationships are not generally ones involving commitment of duration, outside the bounds of the professional context. Consequently, professions (save prostitution, which it may be argued, does not meet the test for a profession, despite its long history as a trade) are not relationships in which sexual intimacies are appropriate. Finally, as a science (some might say pseudo-science) psychology adopts the presupposition of 18th century empiricists that empirical validation is desirable. With this warrant, it is argued that sexual relationships between doctor and patient are empirically associated with poor treatment outcome; consequently, are to be eschewed.

Ethical standards, then, develop in professions both with reference to, and dependence upon, logical — sometimes ontological — and frequently empirical, warrants. Such standards emerge, however, as part of a sociological phenomenon, i.e., with increasing differentiation of the profession as a complex social and bureaucratically structured organism (Merton, 1968).

Psychology is a relatively new profession — arising during and subsequent to WWII; consequently, carefully delineated standards of behavior both developed by the profession, as well in response to complaints about psychologists' behavior which have come before a court of law, have only recently (within the last two decades) begun to emerge with clarity.

The reader may wonder what this abstruse digression has to do with the practice of psychology in rural settings; however, the point to be developed is that standards for professional conduct which emerge in the context of an increasingly complex urban environment with social relationships that, however multiplex, preserve anonymity and maintain social distance between the psychologist and patient, are less easily applied in rural settings. Professional standards — whatever their content — may be no less desirable, but in some cases, more difficult to apply in rural settings.

Standards of behavior which are egregious violations of social conduct across geographical and population lines remain inviolable without regard to whether the setting is rural or urban. Prohibition of sexual intimacy between doctor and patient is likely an example of such standards which have currency across settings. On the other hand, prohibitions against bartering for services may be less applicable across settings.

The *Casebook on Ethical Principles* (American Psychological Association, 1987) discusses a series of principles which form the basis for the APA Ethics Committee to adjudge the caliber of a psychologist's behavior. It should be noted that APA ethics standards exhibit neither the looseness of a "principle" ethic, e.g., "above all, do no harm" (to the patient), nor the precision of a casuistry, which defines very carefully the behavior expected in each and every case. Rather, our ethical standards are in the form of a "rule" ethic, which lays out general guidelines, but which will require some interpretation in application.

PROHIBITION AGAINST DUAL RELATIONSHIPS

Ethical principle 6a (*Casebook, 1987*) focuses specifically upon problems as may emerge with dual relationships that would lead the psychologist not only to be in violation of APA ethics standards but would compromise the efficacy of treatment interventions. Under the general rubric of both respecting "the integrity" and "protect-(ing) the welfare of the people and groups with whom they work," and with reference to the principle that conflict of interests should be avoided, the principle reads as follows:

Psychologists are continually cognizant of their own needs and of their potentially influential position vis-à-vis persons such as clients, students, and subordinates. They avoid exploiting the trust and dependency of such persons. Psychologists make every effort to avoid dual relationships which could impair their professional judgment or increase the risk of exploitation. Examples of such dual relationships include but are not limited to research with and treatment of employees, students, supervisees, close friends, or relatives. Sexual intimacies with clients are unethical.

Such a "rule" ethic is sensible across settings in the context of our common culture; for clearly, numerous examples of dual relationships exist, e.g., combining role of friend and therapist; combining role of customer or consumer of business services and therapist; bartering for professional services, i.e., exchange of services for a fee other than common currency; combining role of teacher, supervisor, or lover, and therapist.

Pope (1988) points out that there are at least four reasons why dual relationships are inappropriate. First, dual relationships offer a risk of compromising professional judgment. With reference to the earlier comments about unstated presuppositions, it is here presumed (and likely so) that maintenance of multiple roles imposes requirements for adjudicating the various warrants that define proper behavior—which are different in different roles. Merely the task of adjudication imposes burdens upon the personal system(s) and increases, consequently, the risk of impaired professional judgment.

Secondly, Pope notes the inequity of professional relationships and the power position of the psychologist with regard to the patient. He argues rather than "might makes right" that power imposes its own requirement for sensitivity as regards manipulation or misuse of that power; as well as the ease with which the doctor-patient relationship is subject to exploitation of the patient by the doctor. This exploitation may be either sexual or financial. The latter has led to a California case (cf. Pope, p. 21, who cites Dr. William Crawford, former chair of the California Psychology Examining Committee) in which a psychologist was "suspended from practice because of a relationship in which he provided therapy in return for construction work around his home to be done by the patient.'' Business relationships, in general, are examples of dual relationships and to be avoided.

Thirdly, Pope refers to a special feature of the power relationship between doctor and patient which depends upon acceptance of the concept of transference in treatment, i.e., that patient transference (positive) with idealization of the therapist has a consequent effect in terms of increasing the patient's vulnerability to any word or suggestion on the part of the therapist, i.e., increasing or heightening the terms of the power relationship.

Finally, Pope notes that the peculiarities of the legal system in granting privilege to the patient in treatment with a psychologist also poses special problems in resolution of complaints, even egregious violations of the doctor-patient relationship—precisely because legal resolution of the conflict would require waiver of confidentiality and (likely) subsequent exposure of personal material in a court of law.

That there are ample reasons for the prohibition against dual relationships, there is no question, however, it will be argued that the practice of psychology in rural areas, in particular, imposes special strain upon this prohibition—not to say special requirements upon the psychologist's sensitivity to potential violations of this principle.

SPECIAL FEATURES OF RURAL SETTINGS

While it is a tautology to say that rural practice occurs in rural settings this statement is a truism that reveals vast differences in both the nature of life in rural as opposed to urban settings, and in the manner in which the practice of psychology must be conducted.

One cannot say, however, that rural America has all the features of another planet. Few would argue that anyplace within America is totally insulated from the information explosion that has characterized our society in the past forty years. The media barrage reaches into the heart of rural America just as into the heart of the ghetto, or the modern subdivision in which mock-French provincial houses are carefully arranged around artificial lakes. While cable TV is not available in rural areas, the satellite antenna is ubiquitous on the Iowa farm, in the foothills of the Big Horn mountains of northern Wyoming, or adjacent to a Navaho hogan which has no running water, dirt floors, and only generator power for electricity!

Just as the media's reach is unrestrained, so the other features of our society, e.g., drug use, are seen in rural America, much as elsewhere — though, most often, the drug of choice for rural teenagers (and their elders, as well) is alcohol rather than street drugs. The scourge of alcohol abuse is not limited to urban or suburban America.

At the same time, the exposure to national media creates a kind of "in-touchness" that transcends distance, providing instant views into tragedy or political upheaval wherever it appears across the globe. As well, the national advertising campaigns create a market even in the most remote areas for the latest video game, doll, cologne, or hair-care product — in fact, markets are often created in rural areas which cannot easily be served because of the lack of proper distribution facilities! Can you imagine trying to find a "Nintendo" game in Tensleep, Wyoming, or Black Rock, New Mexico?

Despite the instant accessibility to information through the media, there are differences between life in rural settings and urban life; differences so vast that they are in some ways both incomprehensible and inexplicable to the modern urbanite.

Parenthetically, it must be said here that the "future" which was likely to "shock" most of us when Toffler wrote about it in 1970 (*Future Shock*, 1970) is now two decades old. However, one of Toffler's predictions had to do with recognizing the heterogeneity of modern culture for he suspicioned that in the future it would not be possible to describe "modern man" or the "modern urbanite" for that matter. Rather, our culture would be a loosely linked republic of enclaves, each with its own features and character. For example, he argued that there would be "enclaves of the past" in which time was almost frozen, e.g., certain religious or ethnic communities, such as the Amish communities and the traditional Indian communities of the Southwest. As well, there would be "enclaves of the future" that would represent the avant garde elements of the culture at large. Modern man is a mythical creature; no uniform description of "modern man" is possible, rather there are descriptions of persons which are appropriate for the community in which they reside. For as Toffler predicted, our culture has become a ragtag aggregate of many disparate elements.

Oddly enough, despite enormous differences, there are also commonalities among otherwise very different settings, such that much of what is written about the practice of psychology in rural settings could easily be said about the practice of psychology in homogeneous, urban, ethnic communities—especially with regard to the intactness of family structures, geographical proximity, and shared community values.

As there is no template for the modern or urban man, so there is no single template for the rural dweller. The gentried farms, and small towns, of northern Virginia are a sharp contrast to a small town in the Rocky Mountain west; and both are different from the rural (by population standards) but art and resort culture of Santa Fe, New Mexico.

RURAL VALUES

Despite the foregoing, the writer would argue that while any description is ephemeral and subtle, there are very clear value differences between rural and urban areas. Harvey Cox (1965) in *The Secular City*, argued that a significant value of the city is "pragmatism," by which he meant a secular, technocratic view of the world. Life for the urbanite is "a set of problems, not an unfathomable mystery" (Cox, p. 63).

> He (the urban man) sees the world not so much as an awesome enigma evoking a sense of hushed reverence, as a series of complex and interrelated projects requiring the application of competence.

The rural dweller, by and large, sees life differently. There is a common feature of life in rural America which binds all residents to the land in a fashion not intelligible to the urbanite. Even the professional: the psychologist, medical doctor, or attorney who lives in town and does not work the land personally, has a bond to the land that is very real and an almost palpable part of the Zeitgeist. Cox's dweller in the secular city can scarcely understand that primeval bond to dirt. Even the most technicologically sophisticated farm manager is capable of a sense of wonder, of magic, and even of reverence in his or her ties to land, that a city dweller might well find puzzling. In the Southwest, in particular, the contribution of four centuries of Hispanic Catholicism and a millennium of Indian culture provide a leaven to the larger Anglo culture, a leaven that is mystical and magical in nature. Weather, a sunset, the mountains, and looking at crops growing, are shared, meaningful experiences in rural America. In addition, it is no accident that in rural areas the most commonly watched television production received on one's satellite antenna is "The Weather Channel," for life quite literally is dependent upon weather's impact on the land.

A second feature of life in rural areas is that interpersonal relationships are more a function of geography than choice. Relationships in rural areas are not determined by intention, by choice, as might be found in the city, but by proximity. Geography is important not only because of the primeval bond to the land itself, but because geography is determinative of relationships—of loves, and of long-standing feuds, for that matter. To be sure there are geographical conflicts in cities as well, e.g., the Bronx vs. Brooklyn, but on a micro-interpersonal level relationships are far different in city settings. In urban settings, in general, one does not (of necessity) socialize, have personal knowledge, nor enjoy a personal relationship with the host of persons with whom one has daily contact, and upon whom we are dependent for the delivery of goods and services—the banker, the cashier at the grocery store, the saleslady in lingerie, or the postal employee. Nor, for that matter, is the city dweller likely to know even the name of persons who live on his or her block!

In urban (or suburban) settings, one chooses relationships with a fair amount of intentionality—not merely because the person is present, whereas in rural areas, the choices for relationships are more limited; everybody knows everybody, and socializes with most.

The extent to which knowledge about one's neighbors is genuinely public in rural areas has long been the subject of humor in plays or films; however, urban dwellers can hardly appreciate the extent to which community gossip is a real and lively part of rural life. In fact, the change in technology and the loss of the "party-line" telephone was a major blow to rural life — precisely because information about each other was somewhat more difficult to obtain (partially replaced only by the local beauty parlor run by "Shirley" or "Laverne")! Information about the size of one's bank account, the nature of purchases in the grocery store, mail-order deliveries from Sears, the fact that the psychologist's teen-age son used foul language in addressing the teacher (or principal) — and the fact that the psychologist's wife came to the junior high school to take the child home for the day — are all common knowledge in the rural community.

The writer can well remember that when the mental health center was located over the community's only drug store (and pharmacy). A trip downstairs to the pharmacy yielded a boundless supply of unusually accurate information about community members — in trade, of course, any customer to the drug-store received fascinating information about the psychologist. At times, this included a daily itinerary for the psychologist's wife who — at that time — traveled a large portion of the state representing a mortgage loan company. ("Hey, Doc where's your wife off to this week?") This behavior was hardly considered acceptable for a woman (sex-role stereotypes are more rigidly adhered to in rural areas), so that much community speculation hinged on her various travels. Certain persons kept careful records as to her schedule — not with acrimony but merely with curiosity.

Life in the city is characterized by anonymity; whereas life in rural areas is characterized by an unusual degree of openness — one's behavior, and the behavior of one's family are not only open to public scrutiny, but become favorite topics of community discussion. This is all the more true for positions of public trust, elected officials, the judge, the medical doctor, the minister, the banker (but not the candlestick maker), and the psychologist. In the city few either know or care about the psychologist's behavior, provided that said behavior does not reach the front page!

Other differences in values have to do (particularly in the west) with the manner in which personal differences are resolved. The writer has observed that movement between social classes is more fluid in rural settings. In the city, and definitely in suburbia, it is possible to avoid contact with the smelly, unwashed, even the blue collar worker — aside from judicious avoidance of the homeless at the entrance to urban transportation systems. The writer presently lives in the suburbs, where all houses have well tended lawns, sprinkler systems, and a backyard pool. One shops at a mall nearby, which has Lord & Taylor, Sak's and Nieman-Marcus stores. The grocery stores are large, contain a bakery, deli, fresh fish market, and are filled with people who are clean, well-coiffed, well-dressed and exemplify gentility. In fact, certain "flagship" grocery stores are carpeted, have a chamber music quartet on Saturday, valet parking all the time, and accept charge cards!

Life in rural areas is far different not only in terms of lack of access to goods and services, but in other ways as well. For example, in rural areas, proximity to persons crossing all class lines is common. The writer can well remember when the president of the local bank arrived on Monday morning with a "shiner" obtained in a barroom brawl the Saturday night previous! That would not likely occur in most urban settings — both because of lack to exposure to settings of high risk (save muggings) and because urbanites resolve differences indirectly, through legal means, rather than through the direct application of force.

In urban settings, relationships — particularly with professionals — are quite distant and formal. If a consumer is dissatisfied with psychological services, a legal remedy will likely be sought. Litigation is not uncommon, cf. the increase in fees for professional liability insurance during the past 15 years, from $90 to $450 per year (for psychologists).

In rural settings, on the other hand, direct remediation of conflict through the nonjudicious application of force is common. The writer can well recall treating a patient who was the subject of much physical abuse from her spouse: The spouse was somewhat annoyed that his wife would seek treatment. He was even more annoyed when his wife conveyed that in treatment she had learned that no person need endure physical abuse. Consequently, he called the writer and made death threats from time to time, and frequently sat in his pickup, cradling a shotgun, parked only downstairs from the writer's office (in front of the pharmacy). The pharmacist would, however, kindly call upstairs when this gentleman arrived — so as to provide a hint that exit over the roof to the rickety fire escape might be the better choice at the end of the work day. Law enforcement regarded the situation with amusement, as such threats (and attempts) were not uncommon in the rough and tumble world of the Rocky Mountain west.

Suffice it to say that the foregoing is not likely a typical event in the life of the urban psychologist, officed in a medical building adjacent to a large hospital!

PROBLEMS WITH DUAL-RELATIONSHIPS IN RURAL PRACTICE

The focus in this article has been toward special problems with dual-relationships as commonly occur in the practice of psychology in rural settings. It was necessary to speak to the development of common standards of behavior and note the extent to which dual-relationships are problematic. At the same time, the idiosyncratic nature of life in rural settings was explored. Precisely the idiosyncrasies of life in rural settings generates major problems with dual relationships.

The extent to which lack of anonymity, and considerable public scrutiny (as well as knowledge), about the psychologist's personal life often creates major difficulty in rendering professional services can scarcely be underemphasized. The emphasis both in training programs and in the tenor of ethics statements is toward maintenance of a certain amount of anonymity in the delivery of professional services. The writer would argue that this ideal is flatly impossible to achieve in most rural settings. Moreover, to insist upon the delivery of services to persons only with whom the psychologist has no other contact would be equally immoral — if not unethical — in that services would be withheld when desperately needed. Consider the following scenarios:

Case 1. The psychologist is providing family therapy services to a dysfunctional family in which father's alcoholism and mother's remarkable tolerance for abuse create a volatile circumstance. The

psychologist observes strict confidentiality so that his family is totally unaware of who might be patients (since many in the town
were). The psychologist's 17 year-old son advises one evening that
he has asked a girl for a date to the prom (an event still held in rural
settings). The psychologist discovers that the girl in question is the
daughter of his patient-family, and that the two youths have spent
some time together—though the psychologist's son has no knowledge of the patient relationship. What is the psychologist to do?
Does he disclose to his son that the family is in treatment and that a
date is inappropriate? If so, is he prepared to deal with the reverber-
ations in the small high school, in the town, and with the patient-
family if the date is broken? Does he maintain confidentiality but
refer—when referral means a 200 mile round-trip to another setting,
and is unlikely to be pursued?

Case 2. In another situation, the psychologist is sought out by his
pastor's wife, because the minister had reportedly developed a suicidal depression. This occurs in a small town of less than 4500
residents; future contact with both parties will likely occur. In this
case, the psychologist has been a guest for dinner in the home of the
minister. Ordinary caution would suggest referral—but resources
simply do not exist. What is the psychologist to do?

Case 3. In a third scenario, the psychologist is asked by the court
to evaluate the mental competency of a felon. However, in the court
proceeding itself, the psychologist notes that the judge and three of
the twelve jurors (or their families) have been patients. Should the
psychologist testify? Would the prior relationship of the psychologist to relevant parties in the proceeding compromise the opportunity of the accused to obtain a fair trial?

Case 4. In still another situation—all of which have occurred—
the president of the local bank (where both the psychologist and
mental health center do their banking) seeks assistance, along with
his wife, in dealing with parenting issues. Should the psychologist
withhold treatment because of the business relationship? To whom
does the psychologist go when he later wants favorable terms on a
new-car loan?

Case 5. The psychologist provides services to a very poor family
pro bono. Because the community is small, everyone knows where
the psychologist lives and the patient comments after several weeks:

"Doc, I noticed your steel gate on that back fence is about to fall off. I know you agreed to see us for nothing, but how about if I fix that gate for you . . . I can't do much, but I can do that."

Should the psychologist permit this activity on the part of a patient? In a similar case, the psychologist provides pro bono services but for years afterward, the family brings a carton of eggs to church each Sunday morning to give to the psychologist. Should the eggs have been accepted?

SOME SUGGESTIONS
FOR THE CONDUCT OF RURAL PRACTICE

Notice that the cases described here do not include the more egregious examples of dual relationships, such as sexual misconduct, joint business ventures with patients, on-going and daily employee-employer relationships, etc. Nevertheless, any transferential relationship would definitely be contaminated by the myriad of personal contacts, both direct and indirect, that are part and parcel of the visibility associated with small-town life.

A rigid view of the role of the psychologist in the settings described would require that services be withheld, and that patients be referred. An alternative, adopting the same model, would require that the psychologist be single, without family members, and have literally no relationship with any member of the community.

The problem with the first alternative is that there are commonly no alternative services. The psychologist could well find himself in the position of refusing — let us say — to provide diagnostic services to a child of a mental health board member so that the child could obtain needed educational services, when no alternative was readily available. Rigid adherence to an ideal professional model might well render the psychologist ineffective in provision of leadership as well as services to the mental health center. Such a position is, in the opinion of the writer *both* unethical and immoral.

The second alternative would require of the psychologist that he or she be but a shell of a person, without identifiable human characteristics. The irony in rural settings is that psychologists who wish to exhibit such features are rarely seen by rural people, because trust is difficult to develop.

The writer would argue that rural practice requires unusual sensitivity on the part of the psychologist toward ethical issues, as well as careful and unstinting allegiance to certain other ethical principles, e.g., truly informed consent, and an ability to tolerate a modicum of ambiguity viz. the dual relationship issue. The 16th century reformer, Martin Luther is said to have offered the admonition "sin bravely," which is not totally inappropriate in the circumstances described; for the psychologist may well have to accept the risks of error, yet act forthrightly on occasions when his or her proper course of action is not clearly evident.

In Case 1, the case in which the psychologist is treating a family and discovers that his son wishes to date one of the children in that family, neither withdrawal from the case nor strict prohibition are reasonable alternatives. While most fathers might wonder about the boy's choice of relationships, breach of confidentiality is not acceptable. The psychologist might well consider taking the issue to the patient-family, i.e., especially the parent-patients with assurance that as the psychologist's son did not, and does not, know of the patient relationship, how would they like to proceed? How comfortable are they in such circumstance? And, if the family is altogether too comfortable, what does that mean? Would the parent's silent permission constitute a subtle sabotage of treatment efforts? Or, would it have other meanings? Depending upon the extent of the daughter-patient's involvement in treatment, and the possible development of transference, is her response to the psychologist's son some effort either to express erotic wishes toward the psychologist, or an indirect wish for parental nurturance, an acting out of the desire to become a part of a *new* family in which the psychologist is the father? Is the parent's delight at their daughter's choice a move to fuse with the psychologist born both of idealization and desire to avoid the more troublesome aspects of treatment?

. Rather than simple prohibition of the son's choice of date, or referral of the family, the writer would argue that maintenance of a professional attitude and relationship is possible — not to say easy, or even desirable, but possible — in which the behaviors of the respective children, as well as the parents, are but "grist for the mill."

It should be added that while knowledge of the psychologist's personal life is common knowledge in the community, to permit more than casual comment or inquiry during a therapeutic session would be both a technical error and unethical. That is, the therapist must remember that despite visibility in the community, attempts by patients to bring into the therapeutic hour personal material (about the psychologist), are attempts to avoid treatment in some fashion or another. Psychotherapy is — or should be — for the sake of the patient and not the therapist. So, if the patient says: "I hear your boy got in trouble at school . . .," the response must be constructed so as to keep the focus on the patient, e.g., "Oh?" or, "What are you telling me?" or, "That information generates some feelings in you . . ." or "What is this, you thought I was the perfect parent?"

In Case 2, in which the minister developed a suicidal depression, the psychologist elected not to become involved in formal psychotherapy; but, at the request of the minister's wife, telephoned the family physician (a young, not exceptionally well-trained, foreign-medical-school graduate) who offered that reserpine had been prescribed for a hypertension. The physician acknowledged that he had not thought of the possible severe depressive side effects. The medication was changed (a cardiology consult was obtained elsewhere), and the depression rapidly remitted. In this case, however, the relationship with the minister and his wife bordered on friendship so that conventional psychotherapeutic treatment would have been problematic — not to say ineffective in view of the medical circumstances. Some tact was required to maintain a good working relationship with the physician, however.

There is a basic principle to ascertain the nature of one's intervention in highly entangled circumstance such as described herein: The principle that underlies psychological intervention is that such intervention is limited in direct proportion to the intensity of the interpersonal relationship. Thus psychological evaluation might well be offered to a child of a mental health board member, but because of the nature of the relationship, intense psychotherapy would not likely be either appropriate or effective. If psychotherapy is entered into, then the nature of the interpersonal relationship is irrevocably and permanently changed.

In Case 3, the psychologist is asked to testify in court and discovers that several present have had a treatment relationship. The psychologist felt that public disclosure would not be proper, but did discuss the issue (without mentioning names) with the prosecuting attorney, and left the judge to his own devices in terms of whether disqualification was needful. It is a matter of no little consequence, however, that the defense attorney was not aware of these facts, nor sought to obtain them during cross examination. However, possession of such knowledge might well have provided grounds for appeal (and reversal) of the conviction that followed!

Case 4 describes a situation in which a prior business relationship existed, but treatment, even around parenting issues, changed the interpersonal relationship. The psychologist did, in fact, provide treatment to the banker, but discussed the potential effect on the business relationship, and secured agreement that any future business relationship which the psychologist might have with the bank would be handled by a vice-president who had authority for independent loan approval, etc. The banker and spouse remained cordial for many years, but there was (and is) a kind of reserve — not acrimony, just reserve — in the interpersonal relationship.

A sticky issue is that of bartering for professional services — both because of the legal precedent described earlier and general disapproval from ethics committees. However, the writer would argue that there are special circumstances which emerge in rural settings in which bartering is justifiable — and even desirable.

In general, the principle is that fee setting must occur prior to the delivery of services, must be fair and equitable to both parties, and must reflect a fair market value for services delivered. In Case 5, the psychologist did not barter for services but agreed to provide services pro bono — it was a matter of personal pride for the recipients (who had discovered that services might, after all, be useful) that an offer was made to provide a service, in lieu of payment. This service was certainly significantly of less monetary value than the market value of professional services. In this case, it was accepted. However, it is conceivable that mutual agreement could be reached concerning the provision of certain limited services in lieu of a professional fee. However, it should be acknowledged that this practice is risky, open to misinterpretation, possible litigation, review by a state ethics committee, and must be—under all circumstances—carefully negotiated *prior* to the delivery of services. Gifts, either of personal service, or objects, have somewhat different meaning in a rural setting where the giver's history and tradition are associated with the delivery of a gift. Even the US Government—which normally regards receipts of gifts as anathema—through the Indian Health Service, acknowledges that receipt of small gifts, of limited monetary value, are sometimes not only justifiable but helpful in provision of treatment services to tribal communities. In some settings, refusal to accept a gift would constitute a severe affront. This is true in Anglo rural settings as well.

In addition to the responsibility for adherence to the APA *Ethical Principles*, in general, as well as the requirements of state licensure or certification, the issue of dual-relationships and the special visibility of practice in a rural setting requires more sensitivity, not less, on the part of the practitioner.

The writer accepts the supposition that personal information about a psychotherapist will, indeed, contaminate the development of a transferential relationship, as well as the development of a therapeutic alliance. Consequently, it may well be that long-term analytic psychotherapy is difficult at best, and impossible, at worst, in the context of a rural practice in which the psychologist is well known in the life of the community.

A principle which follows is that the intensity of the psychotherapeutic relationship and the likelihood of dealing with unconscious factors is inversely related to the number of reality factors in the relationship. This principle will both affect the type of intervention, and may suggest that the therapist will find it necessary to discuss with the patient both the present and potential effects of other types of relationships upon the therapeutic endeavor. As well, the issue of confidentiality must be explored with a kind of explicitness not required in the anonymity of an urban practice for patients will both need clarity and perhaps reassurance concerning the confidentiality of disclosures within the therapeutic setting.

One would also expect that the issue of patient knowledge about the psychologist will continue to present itself during the course of treatment, likely correlated with the difficulty of the issues with which the patient may be dealing. That is, as the patient confesses difficulty, let us say, in dealing with his or her teen-age children, the visibility of the psychologists own off-spring in the community will somehow increase, as far as the patient is concerned! As noted earlier, however, it is important to keep the attention focused upon the patient — and not the psychologist.

The writer would suggest that the psychologist not abandon all features of professionalism; there was indeed wisdom in what we were carefully taught during training: While the opportunity to hunt and fish on the land of a former patient might be intriguing, careful adjudication of roles is difficult in some subsequent time when that landowner again seeks treatment for himself/herself or a family member. The writer's personal experience was that in rural settings, close friends are few, and the wiser course is to keep other relationships as uncluttered as possible. For example, accepting the hunting or fishing offer might be done only as part of a group of doctors from the local hospital, along with the county judge rather than as a very *personal* act which implied a closeness that did not exist and would, indeed, contaminate future contact. Cordiality was maintained, without creation of difficult problems in future service delivery.

CONCLUSION

In summary, the practice of psychology in rural settings requires unusual sensitivity to the effect of dual relationships upon the provision of professional services for despite best efforts to the contrary, dual relationships will occur. Neither withholding of treatment services nor referral is often an available option, so that effective intervention requires open acknowledgment of the dual relationship, and discussion of its effects upon treatment. The efficacy and intensity of treatment will be affected by the nature of the dual relationship. It is perhaps ironic that in some rural settings, it is only *because* of a dual relationship, i.e., considerable personal knowledge about the psychologist, that patients would seek treatment — precisely the obverse from that commonly seen in urban settings.

REFERENCES

Cox, H. (1965). *The Secular City*, New York: MacMillan.

Merton, R. K. (1968). *Social Theory and Social Structure*. New York: Free Press.

Pope, K. S. (1988). "Dual Relationships: A Source of Ethical, Legal and Clinical Problems," *The Independent Practitioner*, 8, 1, 7-25.

Toffler, Alvin (1970). *Future Shock*. New York: Random House.

Practicing Rural Psychotherapy: Complexity of Role and Boundary

Dianne L. Sterling

SUMMARY. The experience of practicing psychotherapy in a small community with a particular focus on complexity of role and boundary are discussed. It is a general assumption that personal data about the therapist is a variable which is under the control of the therapist. What is not usually considered is the relative lack of control that therapists in small communities possess over what is known about them. Also, the therapist is a member of the community, with a visible way of life.

There may be distinctive characteristics of small community practice which warrant particular consideration. Four areas of importance included: (1) The multiplicity of boundary issues that arise in rural practice; (2) The complexity of the role of therapist; (3) The ongoing nature of the therapy relationship; (4) The changed stance of the therapist as an adaptation to the rural community setting.

Practicing psychotherapy in an urban environment is experientially and qualitatively different than practicing in a small community environment. Having worked in the small community of Martha's Vineyard for three years, I experienced a difference in role and boundary when I began practicing in the urban setting of Boston.

It is a general assumption that self-disclosure is a controllable variable by the therapist; that personal data about the therapist is

Dianne L. Sterling, BA, MS, (Loyola College, Baltimore, MD), PsyD, (Massachusetts School of Professional Psychology) currently affiliated with Seacoast Mental Health Center, Portsmouth, NH as a staff psychologist. The author is also in private practice and on the consulting staff at Portsmouth Hospital.

Requests for reprints should be addressed to: Dianne L. Sterling, BA, MS, 40 Pine Street, Rye, NH 03870

105

something to be carefully and cautiously doled out according to therapeutic need and only in the service of facilitating the therapeutic process. What is not usually considered is the relative lack of control that therapists who work in small communities possess over what is known about them. The proximity and community communication channels provide ample opportunity for gathering information about a therapist.

In a small town, a therapist is a participant in the community. A therapist, like other residents, votes in town meetings, goes to the post office for mail collection, takes positions on community issues, and is seen in a variety of everyday and commonplace situations. Milton Mazer (1976), the first director of the mental health center on Martha's Vineyard, described this in his book, *People and Predicaments*:

> For on the island, no resident is perceived as a stranger, and he is assumed to share the common values and the common trials of life. The urban detachment that ensures a tolerable degree of social privacy is not found on the island. For better or worse, people either know about each other or know much about each other. (p. 23)

Another apt quote from Mazer (1976) further sums up this way of life:

> It is not enough that people live close to one another to be members of a community, to partake in one of the essentials of community, they must interact with each other, both in amity and in conflict. (p. 25)

A therapist in a small community is not a disenfranchised person commuting to practice in another part of the city, unknown in vivo. Rather, a therapist is a real person with a visible way of life. While I worked at the community mental health center on Martha's Vineyard, I was confronted with situations which involved interacting with present and past patients outside of my office on an almost daily basis. As illustration, the following vignettes highlight some of my experiences.

Ms. M. was a woman in her mid-thirties who referred herself for treatment due to chronic poor self esteem and depression. Her appointments with me were held at the end of the day, after which, I would attend an exercise class at a local health club. After a few months in treatment, Ms. M. became more concerned about her appearance. After one session, I wrote the case note and rushed to the health club locker room to change my clothes for class. She, too, had the same idea. Not only did I find her changing clothes beside me in the locker room, she also came to the same class.

Another patient, a 40 year old man, was struggling with sobriety and intimacy in his marriage. Since I had known his father-in-law socially, we discussed this connection prior to treatment to attempt to assess the effect it would have on his treatment. We discussed the tenets of confidentiality and agreed to proceed with the therapy. Several weeks later, I was invited to a small dinner party with not only my patient and his wife in attendance, but his father-in-law as well. We had to completely switch roles with context and push aside our therapeutic relationship, since no one knew that I saw him in another setting.

Daniel, an eighth grade boy, had a mother who was emotionally absent and inconsistent due to her manic-depressive illness. We met weekly at my office. One weekend day, I was gardening at home and he appeared, offering to help. He revealed that he often walked by my house to assure himself that I was there and informed me that he had found out quite a bit about me through one of my friend's children, a friend of his.

I saw Mrs. W., a woman in her fifties, for about one year while she was finishing a Master's degree in art therapy. She struggled with identity issues and questioned the path her life was taking. We successfully terminated therapy and three months later she was starting to do art therapy with children. I attended a school meeting for one of my child patients around this time and she was there on the recommendation of the guidance counselor to be part of the treatment team. Again, I had to accommodate a role and boundary shift. These are just a few examples of what it is like to be a therapist in a small community , finding ways to manage boundaries and live in the community while taking one's role and responsibility into consideration.

Virtually no attention has been paid to the practice of psychotherapy in a small community. Sundet and Mermelstein (1983) and Berry and Davis (1978) briefly address the difficulties in applying urban models to rural practice. Sundet and Mermelstein pointed out there are often "urban prejudices" in psychotherapy practice in small communities. They explained that, unlike in urban settings, there are no context-free interventions in rural settings because of the interdependence of the social systems and stated, "One may ponder the profound implications of the notion that the individual and the community both initiate and limit each other" (p. 33).

Though Sundet and Mermelstein (1983) did not discuss the experience of practicing in a rural area, they did discuss the role and boundary issues that confront a therapist in a small community:

> A brief note about role convergence and boundary permeability is in order. . . . In mapping the rural community, one must be aware not only of the multiple roles a person must play (e.g.; the deacon-physician-school board member who is prominent in the Republican party and is on the Savings and Loan board of directors and the CMHC advisory board) but of familial interconnections as well. . . . Boundary permeability is another aspect of this multidimensionality of the rural community, where schematic definitions of social systems tend to blur . . . (p. 31)

Berry and Davis (1978) wrote about the problems that urban-trained mental health professionals encounter in their initial inability to be responsive to the culture of a rural area and stated, "The boundaries of a rural area are often diffuse; as an entity, it therefore differs socially and physically from urban catchment areas" (p. 674). They pointed out that urban professionals must learn to adapt to the culture and expect that it takes time to gain the trust of rural people. Berry and Davis also noted that special skills are demanded in a rural setting such as knowledge of rural politics and power structures, and the ability to develop informal patterns of communication with key community officials. In addition, they thought that mental health professionals should be generalists and have the capacity to work with a wide range of people and be able to use a number of different therapies and resources effectively and stated, " . . . the professional role in rural community mental health should be determined by the phenomena addressed, not by the imposition of the prevailing professional methodology or ideology" (p. 678).

Berry and Davis (1978) also briefly discussed the practical issues of managing visibility as well as the inevitable judgments that will be made about practitioners in rural practice:

> Rural people are well informed on matters concerning the worker's life, such as marital status, family stability, drinking habits, where clothes are purchased and their cost, kind of car driven, recreational habits, religious participation, and residence. Rural mental health professionals must be concerned about their image in the community because local people will judge them on the basis of personal factors noted above and this judgement will color their response to the professional's services. (p. 677)

The above authors only addressed a few general issues about rural practice. Soreff and Hymoff (1976), Ordway (1976), and Mazer (1976) more specifically discuss rural practice based on their own experiences. Ordway (1976) described his personal experiences in practicing psychodynamic psychotherapy in rural Maine and relates them to being in a confined academic setting:

> Carrying out psychoanalysis in a small community is somewhat like practicing psychoanalysis in an intimate department of psychiatry in a closely knit medical center . . . once again because the analyst is a member of the same social group, he sees his acquaintances therapeutically and/or analytically. With these people, as well as his physician analysands, the analyst had to set ground rules about social avoidance familiar to many university departments. (p. 213)

Ordway believed that patients have difficulty in cutting off real-life relationships in order to experience the therapist transferentially. He thought that the easiest treatments were ones in which the patient commuted from outside of the community in which the therapist lived and therefore knew less about the therapist.

Whereas Ordway described some of the dilemmas that a therapist is apt to encounter in rural practice, Soreff and Hymoff (1976) focus on the differences in rural psychotherapy from urban psychotherapy from both the patient's and therapist's perspective. They noted that there is often role confusion and a complexity of interactions resulting from personal contact outside of the therapeutic relationship, and that added information about the therapist affects treatment and changes anonymity. They stated:

> The authors wish to emphasize that the decline in anonymity and increase in multiple roles is an inevitable consequence. As a result of these factors, the therapist will be considered by the patient as 'more human,' more as an individual, and as a multidimensional person. Likewise, the same phenomenon occurs by which the therapist appreciates the patient as 'more human.' Thus, one of the byproducts of these extra interactions is that the therapist is able to observe healthy aspects of the personality as well as the disruptive and pathologic as traditionally only seen by the psychotherapist in his office. (p. 667)

Mazer (1976) reiterated many of the points made above and made many more in his book, *People and Predicaments.* Mazer was the first and only therapist for many years on the island of Martha's Vineyard and wrote a book on his observations regarding the stresses of life on the island as well as his experiences in practicing there. He described the importance of relationships in a small community and the complexity of connections. He noted that privacy is difficult to achieve and that, "Thus, the maintenance of the therapeutic incognito long advocated by psychiatrists for both technical and therapeutic reasons is less possible in rural areas. Such changes have produced situations of stress for psychiatrists, the results of which have been likened to culture shock" (Mazer, 1976, p. 213).

Mazer (1976) made the interesting point that therapists in urban settings become accustomed to living and operating under the protection of a therapeutic incognito and that, "Maintenance of the incognito probably has another function which has rarely been mentioned; it protects the therapist from the anxiety inherent in any vital human experience" (p. 214). He further elaborated on therapeutic stance in a small community:

> Even if the incognito is a desirable stance for the therapist, it is doubtful that it can be maintained in a small community. If the therapist is to live and work in the community, to participate in its social and political life, to have a spouse doing the same and children studying in its schools, that spouse can no longer retain the anonymity which such a stance requires. (p. 214)

He noted that a common concern for both therapist and patient is that a meeting on a social occasion is probable and each is afraid that he or she will not know how to behave under the new circumstances, which adds another role strain.

Mazer (1976) did add some positive aspects to the work – that a therapist has much more information about a patient and can observe the progress of former patients. He also added that the therapist is experienced more as a human being and stated:

> Finally, the therapist in a small community finds that his customary entrenchment behind the facade of his profession and the distance that its prestigious position places between him and others may serve him poorly in his work. His many-faceted position constantly exposes him as a human being . . . (p. 226)

My own experiences and interviews with other rural practitioners suggest that there are distinctive characteristics of small community practice which warrant particular consideration. Discussion of the more notable and keenly experienced aspects of practicing psychotherapy in this context will be interspersed with direct quotes from several psychiatrists and psychologists in rural practice.

Four areas found to be of particular significance and noteworthiness were: (1) the multiplicity of boundary issues that arose in rural practice; (2) the complexity of the role of therapist; (3) the ongoing nature of the therapy relationship; and (4) the changed stance of the therapist as an adaptation to the small community setting.

THE INCREASED ATTENTION
TO THERAPEUTIC BOUNDARIES

When I work with a client, I set some very basic things up with them. You must, living in a small community, set some protection for your client, not only yourself, but for your client. What you say may well be, you need to talk, that we both live in this community and that we may bump into each other at church or at the grocery market or socially at someone's birthday party. We need to talk openly about what I may say and what you may say. For example, I tell clients they may know me as my husband's wife, they may know me from the school community, they may know me in a lot of capacities. If they meet me on the street and they are with a friend, if they don't want to say, 'Hi, this is my psychotherapist,' they need to know that I'm not particularly concerned. So, I say to them, you are more than welcome to say, 'This is a friend of mine' . . . For example, they know that I'm not going to be concerned as to how they introduce me but I also tell them that I will never allude to knowing them in a psychotherapeutic situation. (Dr. B)

. . . You're always running into someone on the street and it is something that's usually addressed in the first session . . . I think the part that's different here is that I always address the idea that chances are we will run into one another at some other place. So you set up some guidelines. And what I usually say to people is that I leave it up to them whether they chose to acknowledge me . . . and like I said, I would even go so far as giving them control of the situation. If they want to come up and say hello, that's fine. (Dr. C)

The establishment and maintenance of boundaries is a critical consideration which overarches all other aspects of small community practice. The often jarring realization of one's visibility within the community, increased information about patients, and increased potential for informal contact with patients all lead to a heightened attention to boundary issues by rural practitioners. A possible reason for this is the unexpectedness and unpreparedness that a therapist may experience when initially faced with extratherapeutic contact with patients. A rural therapist must tolerate being known in a variety of roles and holding vast amounts of information about patients. How these issues are managed could have a direct affect on one's reputation and consequent success in practice. Being faced with these novel experiences appears to precipitate a reexamination applied to the assumptions and expectations of how psychotherapy could be practiced.

It can be argued that urban practitioners could inadvertently become myopic to the assumptions behind their actions, whereas rural practitioners become acutely aware that what they have learned is less applicable in a smaller setting, prompting the need to challenge old assumptions and create new premises. The rural therapist may, by necessity, be more sensitive and alert to confidentiality and boundary issues. Though boundaries and confidentiality are universal and important therapeutic issues, they become a more obvious consideration in a less populated setting.

Therapists in small communities have to create their own rules and guidelines and develop their own means of managing these issues. The principles of practice learned in training are not always directly applicable to the small community context, and only serve as a rough foundation. Thus, for each therapist, the formation of guiding principles of boundaries and confidentiality is done in relative isolation.

Part of the sense of isolation that rural practitioners experience may be due to feeling disregarded and out of the mainstream. There may be isolation in the experience of having the principles of prevailing theories not fit with the realities of practice in a rural setting and one's own inventions feeling somehow renegade and not confirmed, validated or respected.

> Or to put it simply, for example, we have one swimming pool and I can remember being absolutely naked in a locker room and turning around to see one of my most difficult clients and having to say, 'Oh, Hi,' and it was amusing because she said, 'Hi, Dr. B,' not my first name, not just 'Hi.' And I was standing there in my towel and the lockers are too small to jump into but I can remember thinking, Oh, God, I want to just jump into this locker. (Dr. B)

Extratherapeutic contact is a given in small community setting and a component of treatment that cannot be ignored. It is an almost unavoidable daily occurrence in small community living and becomes a routine expectation by the psychotherapist. By contrast, in suburban or urban settings, extratherapeutic contact does occur, but with such infrequency as to make it a surprising and often unsettling event. Extratherapeutic contact becomes an expectable event for the rural practitioner for which some protective measures have to be made. It is useful to consider how keenly sensitive this contact could be to both parties. The patient reveals acutely personal and often painful information about him or herself to the therapist during a therapy session. The patient counts on the therapist to act professionally and preserve the confidentiality of the information given, as well as to tolerate the feelings generated in the session. Outside of the therapy session, the possibility is great that the patient will meet the therapist in a social situation, and the patient is aware that the therapist knows much personal information. The patient has to shift from the patient role to the demands of the particular social context, where the expectations are for greater interpersonal reciprocity. Back in the office, the patient is once again required to shift back to interpersonal non-reciprocity.

On the other side, the therapist is the recipient of the most minute details of the patient's life. The therapist must also shift roles outside of the therapy situation, possessing much information about the patient, while being careful to not allow that to be known. Also, the therapist, as the recipient of information, must tolerate the possibility that extratherapeutic contact will provide the patient with the opportunity to gather information about the therapist which may color the response to the therapist. As Mazer (1976) pointed out, the "therapeutic incognito" of an urban environment can serve as a protective device for the therapist and offers a buffer from the anxiety inherent in any vital human experience. The rural therapist does not have this buffer, and, therefore must tolerate the lack of anonymity and increased exposure of being a fallible human being. The therapist as an individual is usually protected from the microscope lens; however, in rural practice, the lens can become focussed in his or her direction.

The tenets of traditional practice are worth questioning. Current theory and practice are dominated by prototypical traditional perspectives which create a distance and hierarchy in the therapeutic relationship. The stance of the therapist, the 'therapeutic incognito,' could be experienced by the patient as chilly and withholding. Yet patients who experience it as such, and therapists who challenge these tenets, could be easily pathologized within a traditional framework. Generally, regardless of theoretical persuasion, the therapist is usually a silent partner in the process of psychotherapy. The patient may wonder about the personal life of the therapist or what the therapist is really like, but will rarely probe. The therapist, if a shade less conservative in outlook, may opt to share some carefully considered disclosures or personal references with a patient. These are the unsaid but recognized rules of psychotherapy in most settings.

These rules do not readily apply in a rural setting. Maybe it would be useful to examine and even question the rules that are so embedded with us and often taken for granted. Is it so unreasonable and potentially countertherapeutic for patients to want to know more about someone with whom they confide their most private thoughts and experiences? It is curious why therapists are taught to curtail questions directed to them. Being one's self is not often discussed in the literature, though ways of making one's self inscrutable can be readily found. Certainly, the amount of information known about a therapist appears related to the setting. Perhaps the amount of information made available should depend on the setting as well, since expectations may differ. A fresh look at the assumptions of practice may prove valuable.

It is possible that the residents of small communities become accustomed to increased and varied contact with other community residents and adapt to changes in role as a function of everyday life, unlike urban residents, who rarely encounter others in more than one role or setting. It becomes important in rural practice to differentiate the types of boundaries. Revelation is not exploitation. What one may reveal may shift and expand yet always continue to be boundaried by the task of therapy.

There are few training grounds or other settings where much consideration to therapeutic boundaries is required. Confidentiality guidelines broadly address therapeutic boundaries, but offer little additional direction. Didactic training rarely covers these issues since they are often such background aspects to practicing psychotherapy in other settings.

Also boundaries become altered in a small community context. What could be considered inappropriate boundaries with patients in a larger setting may have less validity in a smaller one. Therapists in a rural setting are few in number and are participants in the community. Dilemmas arise on whom to treat and how to deal with the glut of information accessible about patients.

Rules observed in larger communities regarding patient referrals and avoidance of treating patients who are related or connected in some way are not easily achieved in rural settings.

Small community therapists sometimes accept referrals to treat people with whom they have had social relationships and treat people who have close relationships with each other. Often this is a result of being one of a few therapists within the community, which make referral difficult.

As mentioned earlier, perhaps success of treatment in a small community is not dependent on such strict boundaries as advocated in traditional practice. Again, it is interesting to speculate on the success of attempting a pure psychoanalytic treatment in a small community, since many of the tenets of this perspective are not easily followed in a rural context. Certainly transference becomes altered when there is so much available information about the therapist. The question becomes one of how much anonymity and distance in the therapeutic relationship are critical to successful psychodynamic treatment in any context.

The interconnectedness of community residents and the information flow in a community with a small population is another aspect of rural practice that is a departure from the experience of therapists in larger settings. A psychotherapist may be provided with access to a wealth of information about his or her patients both directly and indirectly. Diplomatic ways of devising boundaries to modulate information and preserve confidentiality become necessary. Again, rural therapists are confronted with ethical problems not typically encountered in other settings and, therefore, may have to create their own guidelines. It appears that guidelines set on this issue become an individual decision. It can be speculated that this poses a continuous demand on the rural therapist to be attentive to the many facets of the psychotherapeutic situation.

> At the same time I suppose that some of my training has hindered me particularly because there's a certain amount of discomfort involved in learning which rules to follow and which ones to bend a little bit in this particular setting. There is nothing in my training that helps me deal with a patient arriving at a staff party that I'd been invited to, as the boyfriend of a staff member. There's nothing in my training that tells me about that at all, except in the vaguest sense where I've been told to keep my distance. There's nothing in my training that really told me how to accommodate to such an odd situation, how to integrate the notion that this personal contact outside the therapy setting along with the ongoing therapy. That is something that has to come, in a large part, from one's self and judgement. (Dr. D)

Rules for rural practice are transmutable and complex, dependent on each individual situation. Overall, there is a resonance to the dilemmas that confront rural therapists. Their task is an ongoing process of continuously evaluating and determining the appropriateness of their actions. Berry and Davis (1978) aptly captured this in their statement, " . . . the professional role in rural community mental health should be determined by the phenomena addressed, not by the imposition of the prevailing methodology or ideology" (p. 678).

THE COMPLEX ROLE OF THE RURAL THERAPIST

> . . . You usually don't share intimate parts of your life with people you may be dealing with as clients, however, I've also found that some of the strength that makes you the therapist you might be has to come from who you really are and you end up processing that. (Dr. B)

> People look to them [therapists] as role models for managing their lives and that may not be fair. We all have problems and stuff. The flip side is that it is a small community and there are

by ratio many mental health professionals. You do come to own a role that extends beyond your working hours. This role is typified in the type of model you are for people you are counseling or who are aware that you are counseling others about how to deal effectively with problems, how to handle things and how to live reasonably within a community. — I really believe in role modeling as far as people changing. — That occurs in a small community, that I know from experience rarely occurs in a larger city, just because you're in more contact physically with these folk, that's a plus for them. (Dr. F)

The big difference in rural psychotherapy is model behavior. You'd better not plan on doing rural therapy unless your life is in order and by that I mean, you can have you own issues, whatever they are, you could be getting divorced, you can go through whatever you're dealing with but you must be honest with yourself because they'll just know it. I mean, if you're very basic with yourself, you're fine. (Dr. B)

The role as psychotherapist became both expanded and continuous in a small community setting. This role is a 24 hour a day experience with often no clear distinctions between one's professional and personal life. Information about the therapist is readily accessible.

One of the aspects of the complexity of role is the sense that one becomes a "role model in living" in a small community. Rural psychotherapists are utilized beyond their professional role to provide examples of modeling behavior. The psychotherapist becomes a model to the whole community system and not just to individual patients. The psychotherapist is a known and visible community member, whose personal life is unavoidably more subject to scrutiny. This creates a demand on therapists to be accountable in their actions and to be congruent with what they say and do both in and out of the therapy office and live in a healthy manner to provide positive modeling behavior. One's life may be examined as an example for dealing effectively with common problems.

This role modeling may be further-reaching than one's practice and could be considered akin to a clergy role, where a psychotherapist is expected to behave in a manner that befits his or her practice.

Like a vicar or parish pastor, the rural therapist is expected to hold confidential material and be trusted as a confidante. It can be argued that part of the role of both rural therapist and minister requires being willing and open to having his or her life on view. Both are expected to be active community participants and to be "on call" as necessary. It can be speculated that people use both as role models and prototypes of "good enough" human beings, to borrow a Winicottian term.

It is interesting to consider what it means to be a role model. It is not the role of therapist that becomes exemplary. Rather, the therapist becomes a role model as a human being. How a therapist is and behaves is always paramount — the therapist can be observed in and out of the therapy office. In a rural setting, it can be speculated, a therapist can never forget himself or herself as a professional. Therapists must always be aware of how they are presenting themselves both in and out of the psychotherapy context. The therapist becomes aware that his or her life provides an example and that psychotherapy practice purports a value and a goal for being and behaving. It becomes a necessity to be true to one's self. A therapist is "never off the job" because of the awareness that his or her self-presentation accentuates the practice of psychotherapy as a modeling process.

Perhaps this self-awareness and self consciousness becomes syntonic over time. Consequently, self-monitoring may turn into an automatic and tolerable process. There may be a continuous intensified emphasis upon the observing ego functions of the therapist. Certainly, in my own experience in rural practice I was both aware yet habituated to being aware. On the surface, this appears to have the potential to create tremendous pressure on the psychotherapist to act in a superhuman way and be a vicissitude of rural practice. However, there is the increased opportunity to renounce an idealized and unrealizable image for a fully human and imperfect one. Thus, the therapist can become less invested in looking perfect and "all-knowing" and attempt a healthy integration of doing the work of psychotherapy and being human.

The notion of the therapist being a role model may have some interesting implications for practice. Should we, as therapists, consider ourselves role models? Is this far too burdensome to consider or should we be able to adhere to a standard of reasonable mental health and code of conduct which we could be comfortable about being on view? There is, of course a morality to this that many theories tend to either not acknowledge or try to distill from their perspectives. There are many implications to acknowledging our moral positions within our role as therapists. In rural practice, what occurs outside of the therapy office becomes important in adjunct to what happens within in it. In a rural context, it is possible that our decisions and behaviors become more public, thus, our morality becomes more public as well. It is possible that a rural context demands more attendance to one's behavior and person.

THE ONGOING NATURE
OF THE THERAPY RELATIONSHIP

It just seems to be more of a complete picture that I would see the kids at school, meet their parents who would go to the supermarket, at some point talk to the parent, or see the kid or something . . . I mean so you would actually see, really get into the part of their lives that you wouldn't if you lived in one place and worked in another . . . It felt to my advantage to know much more about how these people were living and it was to their advantage to see me as not just an outsider but someone who was living with them, a real person. (Dr. C)

There's a negative side to all this personal stuff, but there's also a positive side. You know people and you really form relationships with people, these are relationships that really extend beyond the therapy room. These are people you see in the grocery store, shopping for your kid's clothes, I mean you see them in bars, you see them everywhere and the therapy — not the same intense way that it occurs in the office — but the therapy goes on continuously and people change for the better under those circumstances, that's been a real plus.

I've seen direct therapeutic gains to my clients in this setting that I never saw in a larger city. I really think they get better, they tend to have more contact with the therapist, if only by phone or in just knowing the therapist merges with other community members and there's a sense that I just don't see this person and I pay how ever many dollars an hour and then they're gone and that's it. You know, it's like, I wonder if that hour really existed . . . there is something unreal between the hour you spend and then you go out into the city and do your thing. Its like two totally different worlds. That doesn't happen here. I like this much better . . . the personal advantage of being in a small town is real attractive to me. (Dr. F)

In urban practice, the results of psychotherapy can remain intangible. The therapist rarely has a chance to see a patient utilize the gains made in treatment. Consequently, the urban practitioner may never really know if the therapy was truly successful. In a rural setting, she or he is more likely to see the results of treatment and even to have the patient acknowledge this to the therapist after termination. The rural practitioner can experience himself or herself as making a difference. A heightened sense of personal efficacy and impact can occur. It is perhaps this aspect of practice that make the difficulties of working in this setting worthwhile. It can be tremendously reinforcing and rewarding to experience making a positive difference in the lives of others. This may contribute to the increased generativity of the therapist over time as well as a deep experience of personal and professional satisfaction.

A richer involvement can be derived from a practice when one can see the tangible results of one's work and effort. Just as the therapist is visible, patients can be seen in the milieu in which they live and not just in the therapy office. Patients also experience multiple interactions with the therapist outside of the office. Soreff and Hymoff (1976) made the observation that, "Thus, one of the byproducts of these extra interactions is that the therapist is able to observe healthy aspects of the personality as well as the disruptive and pathologic as traditionally only seen by the psychotherapist in his office" (p. 667).

Therapists gain a fuller understanding of their patients because of this increased knowledge about their life situations. The therapeutic process extends outside of the therapy office. Because of the increased exposure on both sides, psychotherapy becomes somewhat more of a reciprocal exchange.

THE CHANGED STANCE OF THE THERAPIST

It's an extremely odd experience, as compared with being a therapist in the city, such as Boston or Cambridge. There are a number of differences, certainly one is that therapy seems to be practiced somewhat differently in a rural area. People seem to approach therapy from a somewhat looser standpoint. That can be good and that can be bad, but I think that clinicians tend to be a little less rigorous in application of therapeutic principles no matter what their theoretical orientation is . . . They might come in approaching therapy in a fairly rigorous fashion and theoretical principles tend to loosen up over time. People tend to just insert more of themselves in the therapy. (Dr. D)

In current practice, there exists a myth of the ideal therapist. The ideal therapist is a lofty being who distills personal characteristics out of the office and bestows enlightening interpretations to the patient in an antiseptically neutral atmosphere. This stance is mythologized and perpetuated publicly — supervisors pass on the tradition to clinical trainees and lecturers and authors tell tales of magnificently curative interventions by god-like creatures called psychotherapists (often themselves). The value is on the finely-honed persona, not the human-ness of the psychotherapist.

Thus, if therapists publicly acknowledge that they self-disclose at times or present more of themselves as individuals in the therapeutic encounter, they may experience shame and the stigma of inappropriateness. Certainly, this is not the stuff in which myths are made. Self-acceptance and comfortableness as a human being do not fit this model. Instead, the model fosters the keeping of secrets. Stiver (1985) made the comment that much is unknown about what really occurs behind closed doors. She related a story about a clinician leaving training and terminating a treatment relationship. This clinician gave her patient permission to keep in touch with her and let her know how she was doing. When she revealed this to her supervisor, she was severely chastised and told that she was being seductive and inappropriate. In turn, the clinician was terminating with her own therapist, who told her to keep in touch. The clinician was baffled and realized that what is usually taught about practice is not a full picture of what often occurs.

Rural practitioners break the perpetration of this myth. They seem to engender a brave new frontier spirit which values the person before the clinician. The myth does not hold, since they are far away from the realm of supervisors and renowned theoreticians. Possibly, because they consider their experiences as unique and incomparable, they are willing to share their outlooks on practice. Though the rural therapist has deviated from accepted premises of practice, direct results of the patient's progress are evidenced. Perhaps rural therapists avoid feeling ashamed since they find that what they do has positive results.

> Early on I made decisions somehow out of sheer panic of having to encounter patients. This was something I had never experienced before because I rarely encountered patients in my personal life in Cambridge or Boston and I would just somehow try to accommodate the situation and maintain as much distance as I could. I think that was my primary objective, that I would not show much of myself. I think over a period of time that it probably evolved to perhaps showing a bit more of myself and in a more relaxed way. (Dr. D)

There is an increased overlap in the therapist's professional and personal life, increased visibility and the expectation of some openness about one's self with patients. Perhaps because of this, the context supports and demands a changed stance and way of being that departs from the experience of practicing in urban settings. It can be postulated that visibility and being known as a "real person" affects and shapes how psychotherapy is practiced. It is interesting to consider the possibility that the "real relationship" may actually help fuel the impetus for change instead of being a lesser element in therapy as it is usually considered.

Mazer (1976) noted that therapists may experience "culture shock" in a rural setting due to the lack of anonymity and the impossibility of maintaining a distanced stance from patients. He added that the therapist is experienced more as a human being without a professional facade. The small community setting may demand some extra thought to be applied to familiar ways of practicing psychotherapy. Some form of transformation is needed—a process of assimilation and accommodation that moved one to let go of the notions and values that did not fit or work in the rural setting. There is a progression from an initial attempt to guard against self disclosure or attempting to modulate how much is known about the therapist, to gradual increase in comfort level with these issues. The alternative of attempting to maintain a less flexible stance and control visibility would require such considerable constriction of activity as to make this an undesirable option.

This adjustment and alteration may have the advantage of facilitating the development of one's personal style in the therapy. Initially, therapists described being acutely aware of their role and how they appeared to patients. Adaptation occurs, not by dropping the role, but by somehow incorporating the role into one's continuous sense of self and melding personal style with theoretical orientation and self acceptance. This can be contrasted to what informs a therapist in urban psychotherapy practice. In an urban setting, a therapist can construct and base his or her role on theoretical models or supervisory models. It can be surmised that in a rural setting, the therapist cannot rely on these models, because neither are wholly relevant. The rural therapist is required to improvise rules and standards that are more reflective of his or her personality and style. The role becomes an intrinsic part of the rural therapist's self concept, which can not be left behind at the office.

Allowing more of one's personality to emerge with patients, including using self disclosure and allowing for some access to one's personal life may possibly contribute to therapeutic gains. This seems to support that the person of the therapist cannot be excluded from the therapeutic experience in small communities. In fact, one's strength as a therapist seems to depend on who one is as a person. A rural therapist is perhaps as much a teacher, teaching by example, as a facilitator. A possible conclusion is that an increased use of self becomes appropriate and effective practice in small community practice. It is interesting to consider if these findings could be applied in other settings as well.

REFERENCES

Auvil, C.A., & Silver, B.W. (1984). Therapist self-disclosure: When is it appropriate? *Perspectives in Psychiatric Care*, 57-61.

Balsam, R.M., & Balsam A. (1974). *Becoming a psychotherapist: A clinical primer*. Chicago: University of Chicago Press.

Blanck, G., Blanck, R. (1974). *Ego psychology: Theory and practice*. New York: Columbia University Press.

Binstock, W.A. (1973). The therapeutic relationship. *Journal of the American Psychoanalytic Association, 21* (3), 543-557.

Borus, J.F., Anastasi, M., Casoni, R., Della Russo, R., DiMascio, L., Fusco, L., Rubenstein, J., Snyder, M. (1979). Psychotherapy in a goldfish bowl. *Archives of General Psychiatry, 36,* 187-190.

Brenner, D. (1982). *The effective psychotherapist*. New York: Pergamon.

Bruch, H. (1977). Sullivan's concept of participant-observation: A symposium. *Contemporary Psychoanalysis, 13* (3), 347-356.

Carkhuff, R.R., & Berenson, B.G. (1967). *Beyond counseling and therapy*. New York: Holt, Reinhart, & Winston.

Chrzanowski, G. (1977). Participant observation. *Contemporary Psychoanalysis. 13* (3), 351-355.

Delvey, J. (1985). Beyond the blank screen: The patient's search for an emotional container in the therapist. *Psychotherapy, 22* (3), 583-586.

Freud, A. (1936). *The ego and the mechanisms of defense*. New York: International Universities Press.

Garfield, S.L., & Bergin, A.E. (1986). *Handbook of psychotherapy and behavior change*. New York: John Wiley & Sons.

Gendlin, E.T. (1967). Subverbal communication and therapist expressivity. In C.R. Rogers & B. Stevens (Eds.), *Person to person: The problem of being human*. (pp. 119-129). Lafayette, CA: Real People Press.

Gittelson, M. (1952). The emotional position of the analyst in the psychoanalytic situation. *International Journal of Psychoanalysis. 33,* 1-10.

Gottsengen, G.B., & Gottsengen, M.G. (1979). Countertransference: The professional identity crisis. *Psychotherapy: Theory, Research, and Practice 16* (1), 57-60.

Grayson, P.A. (1986). Mental health confidentiality on the small campus. *Journal of American College Health. 34,* 187-196.

Greenberg. J.R., & Mitchell, S.A. (1983). *Object relations in psychoanalytic theory*. Cambridge, MA: Harvard University Press.

Greenberg, J. (1986). Theoretical models and the analyst's neutrality. *Contemporary Psychoanalysis, 22* (1), 87-106.

Greenberg, J.R. (1986). The problem of analytic neutrality. *Contemporary Psychoanalysis 22* (1), 76-86.

Greenson, R.R. (1967). *The technique and practice of psychoanalysis*. New York: International Universities Press.

Greenson, R.R., & Wexler, M. (1969). The non-transference relationship in the psychoanalytic situation. *International Journal of Psychoanalysis. 50,* 27-39.

Greenson, R.R., & Wexler, M. (1970). Discussion of "The non-transference relationship in the psychoanalytic situation." *International Journal of Psychoanalysis, 51.* 143-150.

Grunes, M. (1984). The therapeutic object relationship. *Psychoanalytic Review. 71* (1), 123-143.

Hoffman, I.Z. (1983). The patient as interpreter of the analyst's experience. *Contemporary Psychoanalysis, 19* (3), 389-421.

Horney, K. (1987). *Last lectures.* In D.H. Ingram (Ed.), New York: W.W. Norton.

Ierodiakorov, C.S. (1983). Psychotherapeutic possibilities in a rural community mental health center in Greece. *American Journal of Psychotherapy. 37* (4), 544-551.

Jourard, S.M. (1971). *The transparent self.* New York: Van Nostrand Reinhold.

Kapinski, A. (1981). Sorrows and joys of the psychotherapist. *Journal of the American Academy of Psychoanalysis. 9* (3), 391-397.

Kasin, E. (1977). Some notes on participant observation. *Contemporary Psychoanalysis. 13* (3), 364-367.

Kohut, H. (1984). *How does analysis cure?* Chicago: University of Chicago Press.

Lichenberg, J. (1986). The tension between unrestricted personal revelation and circumscribed personal revelation. *Contemporary Psychoanalysis. 22* (1), 71-76.

Namnum, A. (1976). Activity and personal involvement in psychoanalytic technique. *Bulletin of the Menninger Clinic. 40* (2), 105-117.

Neslusan, J.S. (1987). *Client perspectives of therapist self-disclosure.* Unpublished doctoral dissertation, Massachusetts School of Professional Psychology, Boston.

Paolino, T.J. (1982). The therapeutic relationship in psychoanalysis. *Contemporary Psychoanalysis. 18* (2), 218-234.

Rogers, C.R. (1961). *On becoming a person.* Boston: Houghton Mifflin.

Rogers, C. (Ed.) (1967). *The therapeutic relationship and its impact.* Madison, WI: University of Wisconsin Press.

Ross, R. (1985-6). Beyond the anonymity principle. *International Journal of Psychoanalytic Psychotherapy. 11,* 213-218.

Rubin, J. (1986). The psychoanalytic identity. *American Journal of Psychoanalysis. 46* (4), 283-288.

Schafer, R. (1983). *The analytic attitude.* New York: Basic Books.

Siegal, K. (1985-6) Anonymity. *International Journal of Psychoanalytic Psychotherapy. 11,* 183-212.

Van Kleeck, C. (1987). *The curative factors of the real relationship in psychoanalytic psychotherapy.* Unpublished doctoral dissertation, Massachusetts School of Professional Psychology, Boston.

Weiner, M.F. (1978). *Therapist disclosure: The use of self in psychotherapy.* Boston: Butterworths.
Wachtel, P.L. (1986). On the limits of therapeutic neutrality. *Contemporary Psychoanalysis. 22* (1), 60-70.
Wile, D.B. (1985). Psychotherapy by precedent: Unexamined legacies from pre-1920 psychoanalysis. *Psychotherapy, 22* (4), 793-802.

BIBLIOGRAPHY

Berry., B., & Davis, A. (1978). Community mental health ideology: A problematic model for rural areas. *American Journal of Orthopsychiatry, 48* (4), 673-679.
Mazer, M (1976). *People and predicaments: Of life and distress on Martha's Vineyard.* Cambridge, MA: Harvard University Press.
Ordway, J.A. (1976). Transference in a fishbowl. *Contemporary Psychiatry,* 17 (1), 209-216.
Soreff, S., & Hymoff, I. (1976). The practice of dynamic psychotherapy in a circumscribed community. *American Journal of Psychotherapy,* 30 (4), 658-665.
Stiver, I.F. (1985). *The meaning of care: Reframing treatment models.* Works in Progress (No. 20), Wellesley, MA: Wellesley.
Sundet, P.A., & Mermelstein, D.E. (1983). The meaning of community in rural mental health. *International Journal of Mental Health,* 12, 25-44.

From Little Acorns Big Oaks Grow: So It May Well Be with the Practice of Psychology in Small Towns and/or Rural Areas.

Robert D. Weitz

SUMMARY. This article will start with the opportunities available to the psychologist who elects to practice in a small town. It is presented by a personal narrative of the broad growth of his practice,

Robert D. Weitz, PhD, the editor of this momograph is also the editor of the journal *Psychotherapy in Private Practice*, published by The Haworth Press, Inc. He has been elected as a Distinguished Practioner and Member of the National Academy of Practice in Psychology and has been honored for his service to Psychology by the New Jersey Psychological Association, the American Society of Psychologists in Private Practice, the Divisions of Clinical Psychology and Psychologists in Independent Practice of the American Psychological Association.

The author has played a major role in the establishment of the Graduate School of Applied Psychology of Rutgers University and the School of Psychology at Nova University.

In addition Dr. Weitz has beenhonored for his public service activities by The New Jersey Association For Mental Health, Bergen County, New Jersey Mental Health Board, Bergen County Board Of Chosen Freeholders, New Jersey State Youth Guidance Councils, Teaneck, New Jersey City Club, National Conference of Christians And Jews and the New Jerrsey State Senate.

Dr. Weitz is presently semi-retired and resides and practices on a part-time basis in Boca Raton, Florida. In addition to playing tennis, fishing, and gardening, he continues to participate in voluntary community programs and is actively involved in local, state and national psychological ventures. During the past year he and his wife, Ruth, celebrated their 54th wedding anniversary.

The author has played a major role in the establishment of the Graduate School of Applied Psychology of Rutgers University and the School of Psychology at Nova University.

Request for reprints should be addressed to Robert D. Weitz, PhD, 7566 Martinique Boulevard, Boca Raton, FL 33433.

following a serendipitous experience wherein he volunteered to be a consultant to a community board which was being established. The article covers the writer's involvement in a number of volunteer activities wherein his professional expertise as a psychologist was sought, and of the professional practice opportunities which evolved from his volunteer participation.

INTRODUCTION

From the foregoing articles the reader will have learned about the professional practice of psychology in small towns and/or rural areas. In addition to the description of the geographical areas involved, the articles have dealt with several significant problems and issues including ethics, rural values, dual relationships, peoples' attitudes and lack of anonymity. In addition, the articles have referred to problems experienced by the practitioner (and his/her family) concerning adjustments to the community, learning to cope with the physical and social environment, gaining acceptance, relationships created by contiguity rather than by chance and other factors related to living and practicing in a "fish bowl" setting.

This article is intended to demonstrate the adage, "From little acorns big oaks grow" — or to put it more specifically as related to the practice of psychology, the establishment of a practice in a small town may readily reach out to a much larger scale of professional activity. This is what happened when I moved to Teaneck, New Jersey in 1948 (population 47,000) and shortly after established my practice in that community.

THE STORY

To begin with, during World War II, I served as Chief Psychologist at the Midwestern Medical Center of the United States Public Health Service in St. Louis, Missouri. This hospital was a treatment rehabilitation facility for sexually promiscuous and venereally infected females. Its major goal was to prevent infection among members of the armed forces. During my stay in St. Louis I served on the city's Social Planning Board. Following the conclusion of the European segment of the war, the mission of the Midwestern Medical Center was terminated. I was given the option of being transferred to another Public Health Service facility or release. I chose the latter, returning to my home town, Jersey City, New Jersey. In April, 1945 I established a private practice in that city — the first full-time psychology practice in the state, and, insofar as I have been able to determine, among the first three to practice on a full-time basis in the United States. The establishment and activity of my Jersey City practice is a tale in itself, but that will need to be told at another time. Here, I wish to tell the story of my professional involvement pursuant to the move of my family's residence to Teaneck, New Jersey.

About two weeks after I became a resident in Teaneck I read a newspaper article stating that the local governing body voted to establish a Youth Guidance Council. Weeks prior an enablement law was passed in New Jersey relative to the establishment of these councils. In view of the fact that I had some experience dealing with youth affairs while participating on the St. Louis Social Planning Board, I called the mayor's office to volunteer my service as a consultant. Shortly after I received a personal call from the mayor who invited me to visit with him to discuss the matter. The day following my meeting with the mayor, I received a telephone call from the town's medical doctor, who invited me for an interview.

One week later at a regular meeting of the Teaneck Town Council, I was officially appointed as a member of the Teaneck Youth Guidance Council.[1] The following day my appointment was announced in the local section of the county newspaper and later again in the local Sunday paper. This appointment proved to be my professional "acorn."

At that time I continued to practice in Jersey City, 20 miles distant from my new Teaneck residence. Shortly following my appointment, I was invited to speak at a meeting of the Teaneck Rotary Club. I accepted the invitation and about three weeks later I spoke to the club's members on the subject of "Juvenile Delin-

---

1. By established law a Youth Guidance Council would be comprised of a body of seven members including a representative of the community's police department, public schools, and government plus four members who were residents of the community at large. This body was authorized to appoint various committees as needed.

quency." At the conclusion of my talk I was approached by one of the club members (W.F.), a well known local surgeon. He asked me to stop by at his office, as he wanted to speak with me. I did so. Dr. F. advised me that services, such as I had to offer, were needed in Teaneck and to the best of his knowledge there was no other practicing psychologist in the county (Bergen). That observation proved to be true. At the meeting he suggested that I start a part-time practice in the town and offered me the opportunity to use a vacant room in his office rent free. If the endeavor proved to be successful, I could then choose to pay him what I thought would be equitable and have the services of his secretary, etc. I accepted the offer and arranged to use his facility for one-half day per week. Quickly this arrangement proved to be inadequate and extended to a full day and within a few months to two days per week. I was able to make the change because I had a fully qualified assistant at my Jersey City office. The two day arrangement went on for three years. At that time, I recognized that I had to make a decision as to where my full-time practice would be. I chose Teaneck. I gradually reduced my intake at my Jersey City office and asked the few patients who remained to continue with me in Teaneck. They did. Unfortunately, I did not recognize at that time that a psychology practice had value and could be sold. Thus, I simply terminated my practice in Jersey City and established a full-time practice in Teaneck.

Now back to the developments following my appointment to the Youth Guidance council. In all, I served with that body for 26 years, as a member for the first year and chairman for the remaining years of my tenure. In 1962, the New Jersey governor appointed me as a member of the New Jersey State Youth Guidance Board. Ultimately, I was elected as chairman and served in that role for 11 years. These roles brought me into contact with community and state leaders representing school systems, police, courts, political leaders and the administrators of mental hospitals and other mental health facilities. These contacts led to other volunteer public service appointments including the following:

Bergen County Mental Health Board, 11 years, six years as Chair; Bergen Pines County Hospital, Coordinator of Psychological

Training, 19 years; Bergen County Drug Advisory Board, 2 years; Bergen County Regional Health Facilities Planning Council, 2 years; Bergen County Board of Special Education, 2 years; New Jersey Master Plan Committee for Psychology, State Board of Education, 6 years; Hackensack Meadowlands Health Service Advisory Council, 2 years; New Jersey Community Mental Health Board, 2 years; United States Health Systems Agency, New Jersey Region 1, Board of Directors, 2 years.

In addition to the above, during my 26 years of residence in Teaneck, I served as a volunteer with several community agencies including the Community Chest, Mental Health Association, Jewish Welfare Council and the Lutheran Welfare League.

What were the rewards from the years of volunteer public service? The rewards were many. In addition to the personal satisfaction gained from being involved in important local and state activities, I had the pleasure of meeting and associating with outstanding community and state leaders, and further of significant importance, I became well known throughout the state as a practicing psychologist. I received referrals from several sources. Finally, by way of reward, I was honored by the New Jersey State Senate just prior to my relocation to Florida with a Senate resolution which stated as follows:

> *Be it resolved by the Senate of the State of New Jersey:* That this House hereby congratulates and commends Dr. Robert D. Weitz for his long and distinguished service to the profession of psychology and to the people of New Jersey through the manifold and varied professional and civic activities for which he has gained so great an esteem over the years and expresses best wishes for a most healthy, rewarding and lengthy retirement.

So much for the activities that grew out of my appointment to the Teaneck Youth Guidance Council.

While there were many interesting and significant developments stemming from my years of public service there were two which especially brought me a great deal of personal satisfaction.

At the first meeting of the Bergen County Mental Health Board, among the nine members present, I met a county judge, the county prosecutor, the county superintendent of schools and the editor and publisher of the county's major newspaper. Each of these Board members ultimately benefited me greatly in my private practice.

To take one example, after the third meeting of the Board, the publisher asked me to stop by his office as he had a matter he wished to discuss. I made an appointment and met with him the following week. During that meeting he invited me to become the consulting psychologist for his newspaper staff. I accepted and served in that role for five years. Further, at that meeting, there was a second significant development, which in addition to personal gratification, proved to be of major importance to the profession. The publisher asked me if I would like to be a consultant (voluntary) to the Medical Superintendent of the county hospital. As it was, the publisher chaired the hospital's Board of Directors. I agreed, whereupon he called the hospital's Superintendent, advised him of my appointment, and arranged for a mutually agreeable date to meet with that official. In due course, I was appointed as coordinator of psychological training, and in that role, I was able to establish an internship program for psychologists. Several outstanding psychologists in the state of New Jersey and elsewhere have been products of that internship.

The second development which brought me great satisfaction involved a criminal case regarding a man (J.P.) who was arrested and charged with issuing a bad check. Three years prior I had treated this man for agoraphobia. I saw him on a weekly basis over a two month period. Due to his inability to travel the treatment took place at his home and nearby streets. Due to the time factor of my need to visit his home, it was mutually agreed that the treatment would continue with another psychologist whose office was located nearby. What happened later follows:

On a Friday morning in July, 1956 I was preparing to leave for Connecticut to be with my wife and children who were at camp when about 10:00 A.M. I received a call from a lawyer who asked me if I were the psychologist who formerly treated his client, J.P. He went on to explain that his client was falsely accused of issuing a bad check, and was unable to come to court to defend himself due to his agoraphobia. The judge refused to accept the explanation and ordered the arrest of J.P. even if it meant to bring him into court in chains. The lawyer pleaded that I come to court immediately to explain to the judge the seriousness of J.P.'s condition and of the difficulty he might encounter if forced to leave his safe surroundings. Because of the emergency involved, I agreed to come to court.

As I began to testify, J.P.'s lawyer asked me to cite my credentials, whereupon the prosecuting attorney interrupted and said that that would not be necessary (he obviously had decided that I was some sort of a quack who was hastily recruited for the defendant — "a hired gun"). I told of my attempt to treat the man and of the conditions surrounding my personal involvement. I tried to explain to the court the nature of the difficult problems associated with the treatment of agoraphobia whereupon the judge interrupted and in a sarcastic tone said, "phobia-shmobia." He then directed the prosecuting attorney to bring J.P. into court "in chains if necessary." I was then dismissed as a witness.

I was shocked by the judge's action; I felt frustrated and angry. I felt personally attacked. What to do? It suddenly occurred to me to seek out the chief prosecutor (G.C.) whose office was in the same building. At that time the chief prosecutor and I were colleagues on the Mental Health Board and had become personal friends. As I entered his office, I asked his secretary if he were in. She replied by pointing to someone in the doorway, at the far end of the room, standing with his back toward me. About then G.C. turned to face me and somewhat surprised to see me said "Hi Doc, what brings you here?" We then went into his private office and I recounted what had happened in the courtroom. G.C. picked up his phone and put a call in to the man who served as the prosecuting attorney and within a minute he joined us. G.C. immediately asked him, "Do you know this man? If not, you should!" G.C. then admonished him for not allowing me to present my credentials and simply assuming that I was a "hired gun."

He then directed the assistant to have their judge rescind his order or he (G.C.) would grant the defendant's attorney the right to immediately seek a mistrial and thereby stay the judge's order. The order was withdrawn, but that was not the end. The following day the story was carried by the county newspaper with the headline "Phobia shmobia said the judge." I took a kidding from my colleagues for quite a time.

Now more about the case itself. The defendant J.P. was in military service when his father died of a heart attack while walking near his home. J.P. received the military leave to attend the funeral. Strangely, two paternal uncles had died in the same way within a few years prior. For family reasons, J.P. was granted a military discharge. Within a short time he found himself unable to travel in any direction more than ten city blocks away from his home. He lived his life within his environmental limits.

The bad check charge stemmed from a business transaction. J.P. owned and operated a successful gasoline station located just three blocks from his home. He bought a second station blocks away, but still within his ten block travel limit. Upon taking over his second station he decided to change the gasoline supplier to the one he used in his first station. In the closing details, he issued a check to the original supplier of the second station which was later returned for "insufficient funds." The gasoline company, angry for being eliminated as the supplier, had him arrested for issuing a bad check.

Now back to the trial. The matter of the defendant's agoraphobia was brought to the attention of the Chief County Judge. He arranged to move the site of the trial to the police station courtroom which was within the defendant's safe travel distance. Shortly after the trial started, a Vice-President of the defendant's bank appeared as a defense witness and volunteered that the return of the check was caused by a bank error and not the fault of the defendant. J.P. was declared, "not guilty." A few weeks later, out of curiosity, I made a point of visiting J.P. at his home to discuss the matter. He told me that he had made an attempt the night before the original trial to drive to the county courthouse and that he was overcome by his phobia and had to return home. He further stated that he anticipated being arrested for his failure to appear in court and had decided, that if an attempt were made to get him into court forcibly, he would shoot those who attempted to arrest him and then shoot himself.

Months later, J.P. sued the oil company (again the trial was held in the police court near his home) and won. The jury awarded him

$200,000.00 – at a time when money was money. Once again, the story hit the newspaper, but this time it was carried nationally. I later read letters addressed to J.P. advising him that, on the basis of his case, adverse decisions against the letter writers (agoraphobics) were reversed.

So much for that experience. Now what about my private practice? My public service activities in due course led to newspaper releases. On one occasion a not-so-friendly neighbor sarcastically commented to my wife, "Don't they have anyone else to write about?" Be that as it may, I became known to the Teaneck community, and in addition to professional referrals, I began to treat local residents who were self-referred. In addition, I established contracts with five neighboring school systems, three local police departments, two county police departments, one of which included teaching at the police academy and the New Jersey Rehabilitation commission.

So we see that the "acorn" grew into a big tree which existed for 28 years until I sold the practice. I have learned from the buyer that the tree has continued to grow.